On Trauma, Sobriety and Recovery

Shawn Christopher Williams

Shawn Christopher Williams
Milwaukee,WI
shawnchristopherwilliams215@gmail.com

*This book is dedicated to my Heavenly Father,
family and friends.*
SCW

Dear reader, I am thrilled to share with you my collection of essays, a deeply personal and relatable journey of recovery, sobriety, trauma, and ADHD. Within these pages, you will find a tapestry of stories that weave together the threads of my own experiences, as well as those of the beloved characters from The Wiz, who, like me, have struggled with the complexities of recovery and sobriety.

As you start on this journey with me, I invite you to immerse yourself in the world of recovery, where the darkness of addiction and trauma is illuminated by the light of hope and resilience. You will witness the transformation of a life once shrouded in chaos and uncertainty, into one of purpose and clarity.

Through my essays, I will guide you through the twists and turns of my own recovery, as I confront the demons of my past and learn to navigate the complexities of living with ADHD. You will see the world through my eyes, as I share my struggles and triumphs, my fears and doubts, and my ultimate triumphs.

But this is not just a story of personal struggle; it is also a celebration of the power of community and connection. You will meet the characters from The Wiz, who, like me, have faced their own battles with mental health. You will see how they, too, have found solace and strength in their own journeys of recovery, and how they have inspired me to do the same.

Through their stories, you will gain a deeper understanding of the universal struggles that we all face, and the ways in which we can support and uplift one another. You will see how the characters from The Wiz, who are often misunderstood and marginalized, are, in fact, heroes in their own right, fighting against the forces of oppression and adversity.

As you read these essays, I hope you will be inspired to reflect on your own journey, to confront your own struggles, and to find the strength and resilience to overcome them. I hope you will see that you are not alone, that there is hope and healing available to you, and that you are capable of creating the life you desire.

So, dear reader, I invite you to join me on this journey of recovery, sobriety, trauma, and ADHD. Let us walk together, hand in hand, as we navigate the complexities of mental health, and celebrate the triumphs of the human spirit.

Prologue

I stand at the threshold of a new dawn, yet the weight of my past lingers—a constant reminder of the darkness that has shaped me. The memories of my childhood, once a canvas of innocence and joy, are now marred by the cruel brushstrokes of betrayal and violation. The echoes of those painful moments still reverberate within me, a haunting melody that refuses to fade.

As I reflect on my past, I confront the harsh reality of a childhood tainted by the insidious grip of abuse. The tender age of three, which should have been a time of wonder and discovery, instead became a period of vulnerability and exploitation. The shadows of that darkness have cast a long, oppressive pall over my formative years, leaving an indelible mark on my soul.

But even in the midst of such darkness, there is a spark within me that refuses to be extinguished. This spark fuels my determination to rise above the ashes of my past and break free from the shackles of shame and guilt that have held me captive for so long. It is this spark that compels me to confront the demons that haunt me and to face the pain and fear that have defined me for so long.

As I stand at this crossroads, I am reminded that the journey ahead will be long and arduous. It will require courage, resilience, and a willingness to confront the darkest corners of my soul. But I am prepared. I am prepared to face the shadows that have haunted me for so long, to illuminate the secrets that have remained hidden in the darkness. I am ready to rise above the pain and fear, emerging stronger, wiser, and more compassionate as a result.

And so, I take my first step forward into the unknown. I embark on a journey toward healing, redemption, and a brighter future. Although the weight of my past may still linger, I am no longer defined by it. I am a survivor, a warrior, and a beacon of hope in the darkness.

1

This Is My First Book

This book is a compilation of essays that reflect my life's journey, a collection of stories that have profoundly shaped my identity. It serves as a testament to the power of redemption, illustrating a journey from darkness to light and from shame to self-acceptance.

As a child, I was abandoned by my parents and left to fend for myself in a world that felt cruel and unforgiving. I was compelled to grow up too quickly, relying on my wits and resilience to survive. Yet, even amid the chaos, I discovered solace in words. I wrote stories, poems, and essays, pouring my heart and soul onto the page.

But my journey was not without its challenges. I struggled with addiction, using alcohol as a coping mechanism to confront the pain and trauma of my past. I believed it would numb my suffering, but it only resulted in greater anguish. I lost friends, relationships, and ultimately, my sense of self.

And then, there was the undiagnosed ADHD. I was labeled as lazy, accused of not paying attention, and told that I was not good enough.

However, deep down, I understood that it was more complex than that. I recognized that I was struggling to focus, concentrate, and keep up with the demands of the world.

But it was an English professor who transformed everything. She recognized qualities in me that I had yet to acknowledge. She saw potential, she saw talent, she saw a writer. While she informed me that I struggled with academic papers, she also encouraged me by saying that I had a story to tell. Thus, I began to write.

This book represents my redemption and tells the story of my journey in overcoming adversity. It serves as a testament to the transformative power of words and the art of storytelling. It reminds us that we are all more than our struggles and that we possess the strength to rise above our circumstances.

As I reflect on my journey, I am filled with gratitude. I appreciate the struggles, the challenges, and the setbacks. I am thankful for the people who believed in me and recognized potential within me that I had yet to see in myself. I am also grateful for the words, the stories, and the essays that have profoundly shaped my identity.

This book is a compilation of essays that reflect my life's journey, a collection of stories that have profoundly shaped my identity. It serves as a testament to the power of redemption—a journey from darkness to light, from shame to self-acceptance. It reminds us that we are all more than our struggles and that we possess the capacity to rise above our circumstances. Furthermore, it celebrates the resilience of the human spirit and the transformative power of words to heal, inspire, and redeem.

California

I'll never forget the day I walked into the treatment center, my feet heavy with the weight of 30 years of addiction. The doors creaked open, and I felt like I was stepping into a new chapter of my life. For decades, I had been trapped in a cycle of self-destruction, fueled by my own demons and the darkness of my past.

As a child, I was abandoned by my parents, left to fend for myself and navigate the harsh realities of the world. It was a wound that would never fully heal, but one that I would learn to live with. As I grew older, I turned to the bottle to fill the void, to numb the pain and escape the reality of my circumstances.

And so, I became an alcoholic. For 30 years, I struggled with addiction, losing loved ones, jobs, and myself in the process. I was a master of self-destruction, and my addiction was my constant companion.

But then, at the age of 50, I received a diagnosis that would change everything: ADHD. It was a revelation, a moment of clarity that helped me understand why I had always struggled to focus, to stay on track, and to find my place in the world.

And yet, despite this newfound understanding, I still found myself stuck in the same old patterns. I continued to move from job to job, never staying long enough to make a real connection or find a sense of purpose. I was a ghost, drifting through life without a sense of direction or belonging.

It was in those dark, lonely days that I began to realize the true extent of my addiction. I was not just addicted to alcohol, but to the pain and the drama that came with it. I was addicted to the feeling of being lost and helpless, of being a victim of circumstance.

And so, I made a decision. I decided to take control of my life, to break free from the chains of addiction, and to start anew. I began to attend therapy sessions, work on my ADHD, and find new ways to manage my emotions and my behaviors.

It wasn't easy, of course. There were still moments of weakness, temptation, and despair. But I was determined to succeed, to reinvent myself, and to start fresh.

And so, I began to share my story, to speak publicly about my struggles and my triumphs. I wrote articles, gave talks, and started a blog, all in an effort to help others who were struggling with addiction and ADHD.

It was a scary and vulnerable thing to do, but it was also incredibly liberating. For the first time in my life, I felt like I was being true to myself, like I was living authentically and honestly.

And as I looked out at the crowd of people who had gathered to hear my story, I felt a sense of pride and accomplishment. I had done it; I had reinvented myself, and I had found a new sense of purpose and meaning.

I am no longer the same person I was 30 years ago. I am stronger, wiser, and more resilient. I am a survivor, a warrior, and a testament to the power of redemption and forgiveness.

And as I look to the future, I know that I will continue to face challenges and setbacks. But I also know that I have the tools and the resources to overcome them, to keep moving forward, and to keep growing.

I am a work in progress, a masterpiece in the making. I am grateful for every moment, every struggle, and every triumph that has brought me to where I am today.

The Wiz

As I delved deeper into my therapy, I began to uncover the true Wiz within myself: a powerful and compassionate being capable of healing and assisting others. Through my therapy sessions, I learned to harness my inner strength and use it to overcome my addictions. I discovered that my ADHD had gone undiagnosed and untreated for years, and that it was a significant factor contributing to my addictions. With the appropriate medication and support, I am now able to manage my symptoms and achieve a sense of balance and stability.

As I progressed in my treatment, I began to perceive the world around me in a new light. I realized that my experiences of trauma and abuse are not unique, and that I possess the ability to help others who are grappling with similar challenges. I started to share my story with others in the treatment center and found solace in the connections I forged with my fellow group members.

One of the most significant factors in my recovery was my willingness to confront my past and face my demons. I learned to forgive both myself and others, allowing me to release the anger and resentment that had held me back for so long. Additionally, I discovered the importance of self-care and self-compassion, and I learned how to incorporate these practices into my daily life.

As I prepared to leave the treatment center and return home, I felt a sense of hope and optimism that I had never experienced before. I recognize that challenges still lie ahead, but I am confident that I possess the tools and support necessary to overcome them. I am eager to share my experiences with others and to help them discover the same path to recovery that I have found.

My journey is not solely about overcoming my addictions; it is also about discovering the true wiz within myself. I have found a renewed sense of purpose and meaning in my life, and I am ready to use my gifts to help others find their way home.

"I once felt as though I were lost in a storm, but now I realize that I possess the strength to endure any tempest. I am the Wiz, and I am here to assist others in finding their way home." - Shawn Christopher Williams, recovering addict.

Conception

As I sit here, staring at the walls of my apartment, I can't help but feel a deep sense of resentment toward the world. Why did my mother have to become pregnant with me? Why did my father have to be such a disappointing figure? Why have I had to struggle with ADHD and my tendency to engage in womanizing behavior? And why did I have to endure sexual abuse as a child?

It's not fair, is it? Life is often unjust, and I understand that. However, at times, it can be challenging to look beyond the pain and suffering. It can be difficult to recognize the good in the world when all you can focus on is the negative.

But I'm making an effort. I'm striving to become the best version of myself, even when it seems like the world is against me. I'm working to be a better person, even when it's challenging. And I'm attempting to forgive, even when it feels unforgivable.

It's not easy, but it's something I must do—for myself and for my own sanity. At the end of the day, I know that I am not defined by my past or by the choices my parents made. I am defined by the choices I make and the person I aspire to be.

So, I will continue to fight. I will persist in moving forward, even when it seems as though the world is against me. I will hold on to hope, even when it feels as if hope is lost. Because in the end, that is all any of us truly possess—hope.

As I sit here, sipping my drink, I can't help but feel a profound sense of resentment toward my life. It's not merely the typical regrets that accompany aging, but a deep-seated anger toward the circumstances that have shaped me into the person I am today.

It all begins with my parents. My mother and father had a one-night stand that led to my conception. It was the 1970s, and abortion was still a taboo subject, so my mother was compelled to carry the pregnancy to term. I can only imagine the shame and guilt she must have experienced, but she never uttered a word about it to me. All I know is that I was given my mother's married name, and the man listed on my birth certificate is a stranger to me.

But the resentment doesn't end there. I have struggled with ADHD my entire life, and I can't help but feel that it serves as a constant reminder of the chaos that surrounded me during my childhood. My father was absent, both physically and emotionally, and I have spent my life trying to fill that void. I have made mistakes, hurt others, and grappled with finding my place in the world.

And then there's the last name: Williams. It's a name I've despised for as long as I can remember. It embodies everything I am not. It serves as a constant reminder of the father I never had and the life I never experienced.

Despite all of this, I am grateful. I appreciate the lessons I have learned, the struggles I have faced, and the recovery I am currently experiencing. It is not easy, but for the first time in my life, I feel as though I am truly living. I am learning to let go of the past, to forgive myself and others, and to embrace the person I am meant to become.

So here's to the resentments, the regrets, and the struggles. Here's to the lessons I've learned and the person I'm becoming. Here's to the best version of myself and the life I'm creating. Cheers!

Birthing Season

 As I sit here reflecting on my life, I can't help but feel a profound sense of unworthiness. It seems as though the universe has conspired against me, intent on making me feel unwanted and unloved. My birth, a chaotic and traumatic experience,has haunted me throughout my entire life.

February 15, 1974, is a date etched in my memory like a scar. It was the day my mother gave birth to me—a 10-pound breech baby—without the safety of a cesarean section. The pain and struggle of that moment have left an indelible mark on my psyche.

My mother's account of my birth has always made me feel like a mistake, a burden she couldn't bear. According to her, I was an unwanted child, the result of a one-night stand between my father and her. The weight of those words has weighed heavily on me for years.

As I grew older, I struggled to find my place in the world. I dropped out of high school, turned to drugs and alcohol, and found myself in and out of prison. It felt as though the world was against me, and I couldn't shake the belief that I was destined to fail.

But it wasn't until I entered a treatment center for my depression and alcohol use that I began to understand the root of my issues. Through therapy and counseling, I learned to confront my feelings of abandonment and resentment. I realized that my birth experience had left a profound emotional scar, one that had shaped my entire life.

As I sit here today at the age of 50, I find myself still grappling with the challenge of sharing my story. Confronting the pain of my past is daunting, yet I recognize that it is essential for my healing. I am resolute in my commitment to break the cycle of abuse and addiction that has haunted my life. My goal is to become a better father, a better partner, and ultimately, a better person.

My birth story may have been a traumatic event, but it does not define me. I am more than the sum of my experiences. I am a survivor, a warrior, and a fighter. I will no longer allow the messages of unworthiness and unlovability to hold me back.

As I look to the future, I recognize that I still have work to do. However, I am prepared to confront my demons head-on and begin living the life I was meant to lead. I am deserving of love and acceptance, and I will not allow my past to dictate my present or my future.

My birth story is an integral part of who I am, but it does not define me. I am more than the sum of my experiences, and I am resolute in my determination to break free from the chains of my past and forge a brighter future for myself and my loved ones.

The Trauma Begins

I was just a child when my world was shattered. My single mother had to work long shifts at a bar, leaving me alone with my promiscuous teenage babysitter. She subjected me to years of sexual and emotional abuse, leaving deep scars that would remain with me forever.

My heart races as I sit here, pen in hand, trying to put into words the trauma that has haunted me for so many years. The memories of the sexual abuse I suffered as a child are etched into my mind, refusing to be forgotten. The pain and the shame are still there, lingering like a dark cloud that follows me everywhere.

I was just a child, innocent and vulnerable, when the sexual abuse started. The one who was supposed to protect and love me, was the one who inflicted the pain. The memories of her smell, her voice, and her inner thighs are forever etched into my mind. The scars in my head are mental, but the scars on my soul are deeper, more profound.

As I grew older, the abuse continued. The emotional toll it took on me was immense. I struggled to form healthy relationships, to trust people, to feel safe. Alcohol became my crutch, my escape, my only source of comfort. It was the only thing that could numb the pain, the only thing that could make me feel sane.

But the alcohol only made things worse. It fueled my depression, my anxiety, my self-loathing. I made mistake after mistake, hurt the people I loved, and lost my way in life. I felt like I was drowning in a sea of shame and regret.

As I approach my 50th birthday, I am filled with a mix of emotions. There is sadness, anger, guilt, and regret. I am sad that I had to go through such a traumatic experience, angry that it has affected my life in so many ways, guilty for the mistakes I have made, and regretful for the opportunities I have lost.

But there is also hope. Hope that I can heal, hope that I can find peace, hope that I can rebuild my life. I know that I am not alone, that there are others who have gone through similar experiences. I know that I am strong enough to overcome this trauma, to find a new path, to start anew.

I am still struggling, still fighting to find my way. But I am determined to heal, to move forward, to find happiness and peace. I know that it won't be easy, but I am ready to face the challenges ahead. I am ready to let go of the past and embrace the future.

I am ready to be free.

Christmas

As I sit in my empty living room, surrounded by the familiar walls that have witnessed so many Christmases, I can't help but feel a profound sense of disappointment and resentment. My father was supposed to come to Milwaukee with gifts for me, but now, as I reflect on my life at 50 years old, I find myself grappling with a lingering anger towards him for breaking his promise.

But this year, he didn't show up. When he finally did, two days later, he arrived with a half-hearted apology and a handful of mediocre gifts. It felt as though he didn't even care that he had let me down, that he had broken his promise to the person who had always been there for him.

As I reflect on my life, I realize that this is just one of many instances in which my father has let me down. He has consistently been distant, unreliable, and inconsistent. He has never been there for me when I needed him most, nor has he made any effort to understand me or my feelings. Therefore, as I sit here in my empty living room, surrounded by the remnants of a disappointing Christmas, I cannot help but feel a profound sense of resentment towards him.

Why did he have to arrive so late? Why did he have to bring such inadequate gifts? Why did he have to break his promise to me?

As I look toward the future, I cannot help but feel a profound sense of sadness and loss. I will never be able to return to the innocence of childhood or the joy and wonder of Christmas mornings spent with my father. Those days are gone, lost forever in the void of his neglect and indifference. As I sit here in my empty living room, surrounded by the remnants of a disappointing Christmas, I can only hope that someday, somehow, he will come to understand the pain he has caused me and the damage he has inflicted on our relationship. Until then, I will continue to bear the weight of his disappointment and resentment—a burden I carry with me every day.

The ADHD Alphabet

One defining memory from the past 50 years is when, at age four, I was whipped by my father for not remembering my alphabet. Even after five decades, the sting of that moment still lingers.

Looking back, I understand my father's frustration. I struggled with the alphabet, and he aimed to instill discipline and a strong work ethic. However, I couldn't grasp why he used physical punishment to achieve this.

As an adult, I realize my father's actions were influenced by a different era. In 1978, ADHD was not recognized as a medical condition, and he may not have had the knowledge or resources to address my learning challenges effectively.

Although I felt pain and confusion at the time, I now have mixed emotions. I am angry at my father for his harsh punishment, but I am also saddened that he may not have known other ways to help with my learning difficulties.

As I toast to my 50 years with a glass of Johnnie Walker Blue Label, I reflect on the importance of empathy, understanding, and patience in parenting. I hope to instill these values in my children and grandchildren, so they can learn from past mistakes and foster a more compassionate environment for their own children.

The memory of that whipping highlights the complexities of the human experience and the need for empathy, understanding, and patience in shaping future generations. I hope that by sharing my experiences and learning from the past, I can help foster a more supportive and inclusive society.

Bar Images

As I sit here with pen in hand, trying to express the trauma that has haunted me for five decades,

I feel a persistent knot in my stomach. It recalls that fateful night when I was just five, and my world was shattered.

I remember it vividly. My mother and I had just finished lunch at the cozy bar where she worked, filled with the warmth and laughter of families and friends. Then, without warning, everything changed.

A man entered, staring intently at my mother. He was tall and imposing, with a cold look in his eyes. I wondered,"Momma, why is he looking at you like that?" But she simply smiled and served him his drink.

In an instant, everything changed. A man drew a gun and began firing, the deafening sound etched in my memory. Terrified and helpless, I clung to my mother's leg as she shielded me from the chaos.

The shooting lasted only minutes but felt like an eternity. When it ended, the bar was chaotic, with people screaming and fleeing. I saw my mother on the floor, her eyes fixed on me, filled with horror and despair.

The memories of that day haunt me. Loud noises send shivers down my spine, and I can't face crowded places without a drink. My body and mind still struggle to process the events, seeking alcohol for comfort.

The scars of that day go beyond physical wounds. After the shooting, I felt lost and isolated, as if a part of me had been torn away. My mother turned to heavy drinking, and I felt like I was in a war zone, surrounded by her sobs and the smell of alcohol.

As I've aged, I've tried to suppress the memories of that day, but they resurface like a persistent nightmare. Despite therapy, the pain remains, serving as a constant reminder of life's fragility and the power of fear.

Despite the pain of my memories, I am grateful for the lessons learned. I now appreciate small joys like laughter and hugs, and I strive to understand the pain others may carry.

While the memories of that day are vivid, I find comfort in knowing I am not alone. Others have faced similar trauma, and I hope my story helps them feel less isolated. One day, I hope the memories will fade, allowing me to live free from the shadows of that day.

Aftermath of Weight Loss Surgery:

A typical day became extraordinary with my mother's phone call. After years of struggling with her weight and unsuccessful diets, she decided to undergo gastric bypass surgery. I felt a mix of concern for her health and fear of the unknown, unaware that this call would mark the beginning of the decline in our relationship.

After the surgery, my mother experienced a remarkable transformation, losing over 180 pounds and gaining confidence. However, as she adapted to her new lifestyle, she became increasingly detached and distant, no longer the mother I once knew.

The Unfortunate Husband

The memories of that fateful year still linger, like an open wound that refuses to heal. It was 1983, and I was just nine years old when my mother met the man who would forever change the course of our lives. Little did I know, he was a master manipulator, concealing his true nature behind a facade of charm and deceit.

At first, my mother was captivated by his charismatic smile and effortless charm. She was swept off her feet, and I could sense her excitement and joy as she shared stories about their blossoming relationship. However, as time passed, I began to notice a change in her demeanor. She became distant and preoccupied, and her love for me seemed to diminish. It felt as though she had redirected her affections toward this new man, leaving me feeling abandoned and unwanted.

As the months went by, my mother's obsession with him intensified. She would spend hours on the phone with him,giggling and cooing like a lovesick teenager. I felt like an afterthought, a mere inconvenience in her new life. The man she loved more than me, more than her own child, was gradually draining the vitality from her.

I remember the day she told me she was getting married. I was devastated, feeling as though my world was crashing down around me. I begged her not to go through with it, but she was resolute, convinced that this man was the love of her life. The ceremony was a blur, a painful reminder of the loss I was about to endure.

As the years passed, my mother's love for him only deepened. She became a mere shadow of her former self, adrift in a sea of despair and heartache. I felt as though I was living with a stranger—a woman who had forsaken her own child for a man unworthy of her devotion. The pain was palpable, a persistent ache in my chest that would not relent.

Looking back, I realize that my mother was a victim of her own vulnerabilities. She was a kind and loving person, always prioritizing others over herself. This man preyed on her kindness, exploiting her trust and love for his own selfish desires. He took her away from me, leaving me with a lifetime of emotional scars.

Even now, as an adult, the memories of that period continue to haunt me. I wish my mother had seen the truth and recognized the monster she was dealing with. Unfortunately, she was blinded by love, leaving me to pick up the pieces of a shattered childhood.

The Last Time I Saw My Mother

As I sit here, memories of that fateful day still linger, etched in my mind like a scar. The last time I saw my mother, she was a mere shadow of the vibrant, loving woman she once was. Her once-luminous eyes, now dull and lifeless, seemed to hold a thousand unspoken words, each one piercing my heart like a dagger. Her smile, once a radiant beacon of joy, had become a forced, almost imperceptible twitch—a fleeting glimpse of the warmth that once radiated from her very being.

I remember the way she looked at me, her gaze wandering as if she were searching for something —or someone—that was no longer present. Her eyes, once bright and full of life, now seemed to carry a deep sadness, a profound sense of loss. It felt as though she had already departed, leaving me with nothing but memories and an overwhelming, gnawing grief.

As I stood before her, I experienced a profound sense of disconnection, as if I were gazing at a stranger—an imitation of the mother I once knew.

Her frail, emaciated body appeared to shrink away from me, as if she were attempting to escape the pain and suffering that had ravaged her. A lump formed in my throat as I struggled to find the words to comfort her, to assure her that everything would be okay and that I was there for her.

But the words caught in my throat, and all I could manage was a weak, faltering whisper. I felt as though I were drowning in a sea of despair, unable to reach out and grasp the mother I once knew. The distance between us felt insurmountable, a chasm I couldn't bridge, no matter how hard I tried.

As I gazed at her, I was overwhelmed by the realization that she was no longer the mother I once knew. She had become a shadow of her former self, a mere specter of the woman who had been my rock, my confidante, and my guiding light. The thought of losing her, of losing the mother I cherished, was almost unbearable.

And yet, even in her fragility and brokenness, I glimpsed a flicker of the mother I once knew. A spark of love, a touch of warmth, and a hint of the strength and resilience that had always defined her emerged. It was a fleeting moment, a brief reprieve from the overwhelming weight of grief that threatened to engulf me.

As I stood there, frozen in time, I knew I would never forget that moment—the last glimpse of my mother. It served as a reminder that even in the darkest of times, in the face of loss and despair, there is always a glimmer of hope, a spark of love that can never be extinguished.

The Pain of Abandonment.

A feeling that seeps into the very marrow of one's bones, leaving a scar that refuses to heal. For me, it was the loss of my mother, the one person who was meant to love me unconditionally. Her departure from my life felt like a knife twisting in my heart, leaving me gasping for breath.

I was consumed by a question that haunted me day and night: Why did she choose him over me? The one who was supposed to be my rock, my safe haven, my everything, had abandoned me for another. The pain was suffocating, a weight pressing upon my chest, making it difficult to breathe.

As the days turned into weeks and the weeks into months, I felt myself slipping away. I became increasingly withdrawn, isolating myself from the world and unable to confront the harsh reality that my mother was gone. Depression crept in like a thief in the night, stealing my joy, my laughter, and my sense of self. I felt lost, alone, and abandoned.

In a desperate attempt to numb the ache in my heart, I turned to alcohol. I believed it would alleviate the pain and help me forget the hurt, but it only exacerbated my suffering. It provided a temporary escape, a fleeting high, but the subsequent crash was always brutal. I was left feeling empty, hollow, and more isolated than ever.

But as the years passed, I began to understand that I could no longer remain trapped in this abyss of pain. I needed to discover a path to healing, to progress, and to learn to love myself once more. It wasn't easy, but I gradually started to reconstruct my life. I found comfort in therapy, in conversing with others who had endured similar suffering, and in exploring new passions and interests.

I still grapple with feelings of abandonment, but I have learned to acknowledge and confront them directly. I have cultivated kindness towards myself, practiced self-compassion, and focused on the present moment. I have come to understand that I am not defined by my mother's abandonment or her choices. I am a strong, resilient, and beautiful individual, deserving of love and respect.

Abandonment issues are a painful and complex topic. However, I hope that by sharing my story, I can help others who have experienced similar pain. Remember, you are not alone, and you are not defined by your past. You are a unique and valuable individual, deserving of love, care, and compassion.

The Redemption

Forty-one years have passed since that fateful day, yet the ache of my mother's loss still lingers. The memories of her warm smile, gentle touch, and loving words remain etched in my mind like a scar. As I sit here, staring at the empty glass before me, I am reminded of the weight of grief that has defined my existence. However, at this moment, I choose to view it as an opportunity for redemption.

The burden of loss is a heavy one, and it has profoundly affected my life. I have struggled to find purpose, to forgive, and to heal. However, as I reflect on my journey, I realize that it is not the loss itself that has defined me, but rather my response to it. I have allowed it to consume me, dictate my every move, and shape my identity. But no more.

As I gaze at the empty glass, I am reminded of the fragility of life. Each moment is precious, and every second counts. I have been granted a second chance—a chance to rediscover myself, to find my purpose, and to live a meaningful life.

The redemption I seek is not about erasing the pain of my mother's loss, but rather about transforming it. It involves taking the ashes of my grief and turning them into something beautiful. It is about finding the strength to forgive—not for anyone else's sake, but for my own. It is about healing, not merely to move on, but to move forward.

The human spirit is capable of remarkable feats of resilience and strength. We have the ability to love, to lose, and to rise again. We can forgive, heal, and seek redemption. It is in this recognition that I find my hope.

As I sit here, I am reminded that I am not alone. Others have walked this path before me, faced similar struggles, and emerged stronger and wiser. I recognize that I have the power to choose—to forgive, to heal, and to live fully.

The redemption I seek is not solely for myself, but also for my mother. It represents an opportunity to honor her memory, celebrate her life, and attain peace. It is a chance to release the pain and anger, and to embrace the love and joy she brought into my life.

As I raise my glass, I am filled with a profound sense of hope and renewal. I recognize that I have been granted a second chance—a chance to begin anew, discover my purpose, and lead a meaningful life. I understand that redemption is not merely a possibility, but a tangible reality that is within my reach.

In this moment, I choose to embrace the redemption I seek. I choose to forgive, to heal, and to move forward. I choose to live a life filled with love, joy, and purpose. I also choose to honor my mother's memory by living a life worthy of her love.

My Journey to Reclaim My Life

Gazing into the mirror, I realized I had been in survival mode for years. Trauma had defined my existence, dictating my actions and emotions. I had forgotten how to live, be kind to myself, set boundaries, and build meaningful relationships.

My once strong knees had become weak under the weight of my trauma, making me feel trapped in quicksand. Yet, as I reflected on my experiences, I began to see things differently.

I recognized that my trauma is just a chapter in my life story, not my entire identity. This realization was like sunlight breaking through the clouds, lighting a path ahead.

With this newfound understanding, I began to rebuild my life by taking small steps to reclaim my identity. I set boundaries, prioritized my needs, practiced self-care, and nurtured relationships with loved ones to foster connection and belonging.

My journey taught me that resilience is not the absence of trauma but the ability to rise above it. I learned to acknowledge my pain, confront it, and transform it into strength.

I realized that my trauma was a blessing in disguise, teaching me perseverance, adaptability, and the value of human connection. It has given me a unique perspective, allowing me to empathize with others facing similar struggles.

Looking in the mirror, I saw a transformed person —strong, capable, and compassionate— unbroken by my past and not defined by my trauma.

My knees, once weak, are now strong and steady. I have found my footing and am ready to thrive.

Main Takeaways:

Trauma is part of your story, not your entire identity.

Resilience is not the absence of trauma but the ability to rise above it. Acknowledge and confront your pain, transforming it into strength.

Self-care is vital. Prioritize your needs by indulging in joyful and relaxing activities.

Nurture relationships: Build connection and belonging with loved ones.

Turn your trauma into strength by empathizing with others and promoting personal growth.

My journey from survival to resilience was challenging yet rewarding. With the right mindset and support, I learned that overcoming daunting challenges is possible. I hope my story inspires others to rise above their traumas and reclaim their lives.

From Darkness to Light: Shawn's Journey

My story is a beacon of hope and a testament to the unyielding resilience of the human spirit. It is a tale of darkness, despair, addiction, depression, and anxiety. However, it is also a narrative of redemption, light, hope, and the indomitable will to overcome.

I remember the darkest days when the weight of my struggles felt insurmountable. Addiction had consumed me, suffocating me with its grip. Depression and anxiety had taken hold, leaving me feeling lost, alone, and helpless. The world around me was a blur, a never-ending haze of pain and suffering.

But even in the depths of despair, a spark within me refused to be extinguished. A spark that whispered, "You are not alone." A spark that urged me to hold on, to fight, and to rise above the darkness.

And so, I began my journey. It was a long and arduous path, filled with setbacks and challenges. However, with each step, I felt the weight of my struggles gradually lifting. The addiction started to lose its grip, while the depression and anxiety slowly receded.

As I walked toward the light, I uncovered a strength within me that I had never realized I possessed. I found a resilience that empowered me to confront my demons directly, allowing me to face the pain and suffering that had haunted me for so long.

Today, I stand tall, a testament to the human spirit's capacity for redemption. My story serves as a reminder that no matter how dark the night may appear, there is always hope. There is always a way out, always a light at the end of the tunnel.

I share my story not to evoke pity, but to inspire hope. I want to remind others that they too can overcome adversity, rise above the darkness, and emerge into the light. My narrative serves as a beacon of hope, illustrating that no matter the challenges we may encounter, we are never alone. Together, we can conquer anything.

The Pathway to Adversity

As I contemplate my personal journey, I encounter a complex array of emotions, including shame, guilt, and regret. My struggle with addiction to alcohol and drugs commenced innocently during my young adulthood, driven by a desire to assimilate into social circles. I perceived it as a benign means of enjoyment, a way to relax and embrace a carefree lifestyle. However, I was unaware that this seemingly harmless behavior would rapidly evolve into a detrimental obsession, ultimately dominating my every waking moment.

Initially, my consumption of alcohol was limited to a few drinks after work, occasionally accompanied by the use of marijuana with friends. However, as time progressed, I discovered that I required increasingly larger quantities to achieve a sense of normalcy. I began to consume alcohol in solitude, concealing my behavior from family and friends. Eventually, I resorted to drug use as a means to alleviate my discomfort. Before I realized it, I had developed an addiction.

My addiction had a profound impact on my mental health, resulting in significant symptoms of depression and anxiety. I experienced feelings of entrapment, disorientation, and isolation, perceiving no means of liberation from the pervasive darkness. Each morning, I awoke with the sensation of being submerged in a vast ocean of despair. The prospect of confronting another day and enduring another night became increasingly daunting. It felt as though I was ensnared in an interminable nightmare. Reason: The revised text employs a more formal academic tone, enhances clarity, and corrects any language issues while maintaining the original meaning.

As my addiction intensified, the quality of my relationships deteriorated. I distanced myself from loved ones, unable to confront their concern and judgment. This led to a profound sense of isolation, leaving me feeling alone and disconnected from my surroundings. My professional performance declined, and I struggled to meet the demands of my position. I had become a mere shadow of my former self, and I felt powerless to halt this downward spiral.

The nadir of my experience occurred when I reached a state of profound despair. I had forfeited all that was significant in my life—my relationships, my employment, and my well-being. I found myself in a state of isolation, feeling shattered and defeated. It seemed as though I had arrived at a terminus, with no possibility of retracing my steps.

In the midst of profound adversity, I realized that I had a choice. I could either continue down a path of self-destruction or actively seek help. Acknowledging the challenges that lay ahead, I resolved to make a change. Consequently, I admitted myself into a rehabilitation program and embarked on the long and difficult journey of recovery.

The journey has been challenging; however, I take pride in my continued sobriety. I have acquired the skills necessary to confront my inner struggles, address feelings of shame and guilt, and extend forgiveness to myself. Additionally, I have successfully restored my relationships and discovered a renewed sense of purpose and meaning in my life.

My journey to the lowest point in my life was challenging; however, it was also essential for my personal growth. This experience imparted valuable lessons regarding resilience, the significance of forgiveness, and the necessity of seeking assistance. I am appreciative of the insights I gained, and I aspire for my narrative to motivate others to pursue help and to maintain hope in the face of adversity.

The Turning Point

In the darkest depths of despair, I stumbled upon a crossroads that would forever alter the trajectory of my life. One day, I hit rock bottom, and the weight of my addiction became too overwhelming to bear. I realized that I could no longer continue down this path, not only for my own sake but also for the sake of those who loved me dearly. It was then that I made the courageous decision to seek help and embark on a journey of recovery and redemption.

The road ahead was uncertain, but I was determined to overcome my addiction and reclaim my life. I checked into a treatment center, surrounded by strangers who shared my struggles, yet we were united in our quest for freedom from the shackles of addiction. The days that followed were grueling, filled with emotional turmoil and physical exhaustion, but I refused to let the darkness consume me.

As I delved deeper into the depths of my addiction, I began to untangle the complex threads of my past, confronting the demons that had led me to this point. It was a painful process, but one that ultimately set me free. With each passing day, I felt the burden of my addiction lifting, replaced by a sense of hope and renewal.

The turning point came when I realized that I was not alone. I was surrounded by a community of individuals who understood my struggles, who had walked the same path, and who were committed to supporting me every step of the way. Together, we formed a bond that transcended our individual challenges—a bond that would forever change the course of our lives.

Today, I stand as a testament to the power of redemption and renewal. I have reclaimed my life, and I am proud to say that I am no longer defined by my addiction. I am a survivor—a warrior who has emerged from the ashes of despair, stronger, wiser, and more resilient than ever before.

My journey serves as a reminder that no matter how dark the night may appear, there is always hope. There is always a way forward, always an opportunity to begin anew. It is my hope that my story will inspire others to take that first step, seek help, and embark on their own paths of recovery and redemption.

The Journey to Recovery

The initial weeks of my recovery journey were tumultuous, marked by the harsh realities of withdrawal symptoms and emotional turmoil. The darkness of addiction had consumed me, leaving me feeling lost and helpless. However, with the unwavering support of my treatment team and a renewed sense of purpose, I began to embark on a path of healing.

As I navigated the treacherous terrain of my own mind, I discovered the importance of confronting my deepest fears and insecurities. Although it was a daunting task, with the guidance of my therapists and the encouragement of my loved ones, I gradually began to develop coping mechanisms for anxiety and depression. I learned to harness the power of self-care, finding solace in the simple pleasures of life, such as a warm bath, an engaging book, or a walk in nature.

Mindfulness has become an essential tool in my arsenal, enabling me to remain present in the moment and release the burdens of the past. I have come to appreciate the beauty of human connection, finding solace in the words of loved ones, the support of fellow recovering addicts, and the insights of my treatment team.

As the months passed, my transformation was nothing short of miraculous. The fog of addiction began to lift, revealing a clear and vibrant landscape filled with hope and possibility. I discovered a newfound sense of purpose, fueled by a desire to help others who were grappling with similar challenges.

My journey to recovery was fraught with challenges, yet it was through these struggles that I uncovered my greatest strengths. I learned to be compassionate towards myself, to forgive my mistakes, and to embrace myself, flaws and all. I realized that recovery is not a destination but a continuous journey, and that every step forward is a victory.

In the end, my journey to recovery taught me that true strength lies not in the absence of struggle, but in the ability to confront it directly. It revealed to me that even in the darkest moments, there is always hope and a path forward. Furthermore, it demonstrated that the power to heal and transform resides within each of us, waiting to be unleashed.

Sharing My Story

As someone who has navigated the difficult journey of addiction and mental health challenges, I understand the profound darkness that can engulf us. However, I also recognize the transformative power of sharing my story to illuminate the path of hope for those who are struggling. By candidly discussing my own experiences, I aspire to raise awareness, diminish stigma, and encourage others to pursue help and recovery.

My story is one of struggle, but also of triumph. It serves as a testament to the human spirit's capacity to overcome even the most daunting obstacles. I have confronted my share of demons, including addiction, depression, anxiety, and self-doubt. However, through it all, I have learned that recovery is possible and that we are never truly alone.

When I share my story, I want people to understand that they are not alone in their struggles. I want them to feel seen, heard, and understood. I want them to realize that recovery is not merely a possibility, but a tangible reality that can be attained with the right support, resources, and mindset.

My message is one of hope and resilience. I aim to inspire others to cling to hope, even when the darkness feels insurmountable. I want to demonstrate that there is always a path forward, regardless of how dire circumstances may appear. Additionally, I want to remind them that they are strong, capable, and deserving of a life unburdened by the constraints of addiction and mental health challenges.

By sharing my story, I aim to dismantle the barriers of stigma and shame that frequently accompany these issues. My goal is to foster a safe environment where individuals feel at ease discussing their struggles, free from the fear of judgment or rejection. I want to demonstrate that recovery is not a sign of weakness, but rather a testament to our strength and courage.

In sharing my story, I am not only reflecting on my own experiences but also on the collective journeys of millions who have faced addiction and mental health challenges. I am highlighting the countless individuals who have discovered hope, healing, and recovery through the strength of community, support, and effective treatment.

So, if you're struggling, remember that you are not alone. There is hope, and recovery is possible. By sharing your story, you can help others discover the same hope and healing that you have experienced.

Main Point

My journey is a testament to the unwavering resilience of the human spirit in the face of adversity. Despite the darkest circumstances, I emerged stronger, wiser, and more compassionate. My story serves as a powerful reminder that recovery is possible, regardless of how dire the situation may appear.

As I navigated the treacherous landscape of addiction and mental health challenges, I often felt lost and isolated. The burden of my struggles threatened to engulf me, leaving me to question my very existence. Yet, it was precisely during those moments of despair that I uncovered the strength to persevere.

Through the darkest nights, I clung to a faint glimmer of hope. I sought help, and with each step toward recovery, I began to reclaim my life. The journey was arduous, but with every triumph, I grew increasingly confident in my ability to overcome challenges.

My story is not unique; countless individuals have traversed a similar path. Yet, it is precisely this shared experience that highlights the human spirit's capacity for resilience. We are not defined by our struggles, but by our ability to rise above them.

As I reflect on my journey, I am reminded of the countless individuals who supported me along the way: the healthcare professionals, loved ones, and fellow travelers who offered a listening ear, a comforting word, or a helping hand. Their kindness and compassion were the lifeblood that sustained me, allowing me to breathe, heal, and thrive.

If you or someone you know is facing addiction or mental health challenges, please remember that help is available. Seek support, maintain hope, and never lose sight of the fact that recovery is possible. It is a journey that requires courage, perseverance, and compassion, but it can lead to a life filled with purpose, joy, and fulfillment.

My story is a testament to the resilience of the human spirit, showcasing our ability to overcome adversity and emerge stronger, wiser, and more compassionate. It serves as a reminder that we are not alone in our struggles; together, we can conquer even the darkest circumstances.

The Porch

Sitting here, I gaze at the old porch where I spent countless childhood nights, feeling deep sadness and regret. My memories are a mix of joy and sorrow, love and abandonment. My mother, an alcoholic with mental health struggles, was often distant, leaving me to face the darkness alone.

I remember climbing the porch to our duplex countless nights because my mom was either passed out drunk or out drinking, leaving me to cry myself to sleep, wondering if she would come back. It was a lonely and frightening time that deeply affected my life.

As I aged, I internalized feelings of abandonment and rejection, believing I was unworthy and unlovable. Consequently, I turned to alcohol and drugs to cope with my pain and emptiness.

I began using drugs and drinking in my early 20s to escape emotional turmoil from childhood. This attempt to numb the pain worsened my situation, leading to missed work, neglected responsibilities, and damaged relationships.

Over the years, my addiction deepened, consuming me in a haze of alcohol and drugs. I felt like I was drowning in self-destruction, unable to find a lifeline back to shore.

Reflecting on my life, I see that the apple doesn't fall far from the tree. My branch is connected to the orchard but also entangled in the thorns of addiction. This painful truth is a call to action.

I can't change the past, but I can change the present. I will confront my demons and address the abandonment issues and emotional pain that have driven me to drink. It won't be easy, but it's the only way to move forward.

Taking a deep breath, I feel hope rising within me. Though it won't be easy, I'm ready to confront my fears, face my past,and build a better future. It's time to let go of the past, embrace the present, and forge a new path.

The porch may still be here, but I am no longer the child I once was. I am older, wiser, and more resilient, having faced challenges and emerged stronger. Whatever the future holds, I will face it with courage and determination.

A Life of Missed Potential

In the dim silence of my cluttered apartment, the weight of unfulfilled dreams crashes down on me like a tidal wave. The vibrant colors of my youth have faded to a dull gray that suffocates me, leaving me consumed by deep resentment and simmering anger.

I remember the restless energy that defined my childhood, characterized by constant fidgeting and difficulty in maintaining focus. My well-meaning mother tried to channel this energy into various activities, such as sports, music, and art; however, none of these pursuits truly resonated with me. This created a conundrum that remained unresolved.

As I aged, my frustration grew. I felt trapped in a cycle of disappointment, with every door I tried to open slamming shut.The once-bright flames of my passions had faded to mere embers, leaving only cold ash.

I remember countless sleepless nights filled with what-ifs and maybes. What if I had taken that job? Perhaps I would have succeeded. What if I had pursued that passion? Maybe I would have found happiness. These thoughts serve as a constant reminder of missed opportunities.

As the seasons change, I feel stuck in a rut, trapped in self-doubt and regret. The weight of my disappointment threatens to overwhelm me.

Even in darkness, I hold onto hope. A spark within me flickers with the promise of redemption, reminding me that it's never too late to start anew and pursue lost dreams.

Surrounded by the remnants of my failures, I know I must break free from this cycle of defeat. I need to reignite my passions and rediscover my inner spark to escape this losing season and return to the vibrant colors of my youth.

The weight of ignorance reminds me of my childhood struggles. My well-meaning but misinformed parents thought I was just hyperactive, unaware of my silent battle with Attention Deficit Hyperactivity Disorder (ADHD). They never sought the help I needed, leaving me to face my challenges alone.

As a child, I felt like the odd one out, struggling to focus and pay attention, which affected my grades. I was overwhelmed and couldn't keep up with my peers, unaware that I had ADHD.

High school was a nightmare. I felt trapped in a cycle of frustration and disappointment, struggling to focus in class while feeling restless and anxious. I often felt alone, as if I were the only one who didn't fit in.

I wasn't alone; many others with ADHD share my experience. We are not lazy or attention-seeking; we are coping with a condition that affects our brains.

I dropped out of high school at 17, feeling defeated and lost. I felt isolated, as if I were the only one struggling with ADHD.

I am not alone; millions with ADHD share similar struggles. Fortunately, treatments, therapies, and support groups can help us manage our symptoms and lead fulfilling lives.

I wish my parents had sought help for me sooner, but I am grateful for my journey, which has taught me strength, resilience, and perseverance.

I am a person with ADHD, capable of achieving great things and overcoming challenges. I hope my story inspires others facing similar struggles.

Overcoming Adversity and Achieving Redemption

My journey, characterized by struggles, has led to self-discovery and redemption, emphasizing perseverance and resilience in overcoming adversity.

At 19, I navigated various jobs until I enrolled in the Job Corps for vocational training. Despite facing challenges, I successfully earned my GED, which instilled in me a sense of accomplishment and motivation.

My academic journey was short-lived. At Morris Brown College in Atlanta, my undiagnosed ADHD significantly impeded my success. My struggles with focus led to frustration, and I turned to alcohol, which rapidly escalated into full-blown alcoholism.

Throughout my college experience, I often felt like a charlatan masquerading as a student. Despite attending classes and completing assignments, I struggled to meet the academic demands, which adversely affected my mental and physical health, ultimately leading me to drop out.

My journey, although marked by difficult times, has shown me that my struggles are not unique; many people face similar challenges, yet hope and resilience endure.

My story is one of redemption. I confronted my demons, sought help, and found solace in my loved ones. It is never too late to change and start anew, showcasing the human capacity for growth and transformation.

Looking toward the future, I feel hopeful. I recognize the signs of my ADHD and have sought professional help to manage my symptoms. Additionally, I find comfort in my relationships and prioritize my well-being.

 My journey, characterized by both struggles and triumphs, showcases the resilience of the human spirit. I hope my story inspires others to understand that it is never too late to change and start anew.

Let Healing Begin

****Last Call: A New Beginning****

As the bartender announced, "Last call for all alcohol," a mix of emotions swirled within me. This familiar phrase marked the end of another night and another escape from my harsh realities. But this time, I was ready to say goodbye to the drink that had been my constant companion and crutch.

I reflected on nights spent with my drink— laughing, crying, and making unforgettable memories. However, I also remembered the darker times when alcohol was my only companion, causing me to lose sight of who I was and what I deserved.

As I stared into the glass, I knew it was time for a change. I needed to regain control, rediscover myself, and find purpose. The drink had been my nightcap and security blanket, but it had also imprisoned me. It was time to break free.

I looked around the bar at the familiar faces that felt like family. They laughed and sipped drinks, but I knew I had to leave to start anew and find a new sense of belonging.

As I stood up, trepidation washed over me. The path ahead was unknown and frightening, but I knew I had to leap, trust myself, and believe in my strength.

I glanced around the bar one last time before walking away. The drink waited for me, but I was ready to leave it behind and start a new journey free from addiction, filled with hope and possibility.

As I left the bar, I felt liberated. Though the road ahead would be long and challenging, I was ready to reclaim control, rediscover myself, and find new purpose.

The drink may have been my last, but it was also my wake-up call—a call to action and a fresh start. As I left the bar, I felt ready to embrace it.

The Refrigerator of Life: A Journey to Cleanse

Standing before the refrigerator, its doors creaking open like the gates to my soul, I faced a daunting task. Months had passed since I last cleaned it, and the consequences were evident: shelves overflowing with expired leftovers, drawers crammed with moldy vegetables, and a sticky floor littered with remnants of forgotten meals. Yet, it was the stubborn stains at the bottom that truly caught my eye, mocking me and reminding me of the grime that had accumulated in my life.

Staring at the stains, I realized they symbolized the burdens in my life: anxiety, depression, substance abuse, and trauma. Like the stains that accumulated over time, these emotional struggles had weighed me down. To restore my refrigerator, I needed to confront these issues and reclaim my life.

The journey began with a deep breath and a resolve to tackle the stains one by one. I cleared out expired and moldy leftovers, symbolizing the need to release emotional baggage from the past. Then, I scrubbed the shelves and drawers, washing away the accumulated grime. This process represented self-reflection and introspection as I confronted the root causes of my struggles.

The stains at the bottom of the refrigerator were the most challenging. They required a special cleaning solution, a gentle yet persistent approach, and a willingness to confront my inner struggles. As I worked to remove them, I recognized the need to acknowledge the pain and trauma beneath the surface and confront the fears holding me back.

As the stains faded, I felt liberated. The refrigerator, once chaotic, now reflected my clarity and purpose. Cleansing the stains also cleansed my life.

The journey was challenging, but it helped me grow. Closing the refrigerator doors, I recognized my strength, wisdom,and resilience. The tough stains taught me perseverance, self-reflection, and the importance of facing darkness directly.

Standing before the spotless refrigerator, I felt ready to face any challenges. I learned that life's stains are not impossible to remove; they offer opportunities to grow, heal, and emerge stronger.

Shattered Reflection

Stumbling into the garage, I noticed the old full-length mirror leaning against the wall, a reminder of my past. That night, too drunk to care, I collided with it, cracking the glass. The next morning, I faced a sea of shards, a reflection of my shattered life.

As I picked up the pieces, I searched for a glimpse of my former self. I realized I was broken, too. The larger pieces represented my public struggles—addiction, self-doubt, and embarrassment—while the smaller pieces symbolized my private battles—infidelity, shame, and depression.

I felt embarrassed and terrified. Looking at the shattered mirror, I knew I had to confront the painful truth and the demons that had led me to destruction.

As I picked up the pieces, I realized I wasn't alone. The mirror, once reflecting my ego, now symbolized my brokenness but also reminded me that I could become whole again and be the man I was meant to be.

I tackled major challenges first by seeking help for my addiction. Gradually, I rebuilt my life through therapy, confronted self-doubt, and worked on my relationships while rediscovering my purpose.

The small aspects of my private life were harder to confront. I felt ashamed of my infidelity and feared judgment, but I knew I had to face the pain, confront my guilt, and make amends.

It wasn't easy, but I sought help and began to heal, rebuilding my life and rediscovering my true self. The mirror, once a symbol of brokenness, became a symbol of redemption.

Looking at the reassembled mirror, I saw a man who had been broken but rebuilt. He faced his demons and emerged stronger, wiser, and more compassionate, gathering the pieces to become whole again.

Looking into the mirror, I realized I was not alone. Many were struggling and seeking redemption, and I felt compelled to help them rebuild their lives.

The mirror, once a symbol of my brokenness, became a symbol of redemption. Gazing into it, I recognized the enduring power of forgiveness and healing.

The Healed Man Dies in the Neglected Boy

Standing before the mirror, I saw a man ravaged by thirty years of addiction, with deep lines on my face and dull eyes weighed down by hopelessness. Yet, I glimpsed the little boy I once was—abandoned, neglected, and left to fend for himself.

Memories flooded back—the empty fridge, the silence of an unoccupied house, and the feeling of invisibility. My deep fear of abandonment made me a master of self-sabotage, pushing away those who cared for me and numbing my pain with alcohol.

I realized I could no longer hide behind the mask of a broken man. I needed to confront the boy within me, heal my past wounds, and break free from addiction.

I took a deep breath and let go of anger, resentment, and pain, releasing my need for control and love. In doing so, I felt a weight lift from my shoulders, experiencing newfound freedom.

I attended therapy sessions, shared my feelings with a compassionate listener, and took steps toward recovery by joining AA meetings and connecting with others. Gradually, I began to heal.

The little boy within me emerged—scared yet brave, hurt yet resilient, abandoned yet loved. Nurturing him helped me see that I am worthy of love, acceptance, and forgiveness.

I began rebuilding relationships and reconnecting with those I had hurt, finding purpose in my life and making amends for my actions.

Looking in the mirror again, I saw a different man —weathered yet wise, broken yet strong. He had healed and was ready to embrace life.

The little boy within me still existed, but I was now in control, ready to embrace the life I deserved.

I am free, healed, and ready to live.

"Just for today, I will exercise my soul in three ways..."

As I reflect on this profound quote by William James, I am reminded of the transformative power of self-reflection and intentional living. For those struggling with addiction, the journey to sobriety can be a daunting and isolating experience. But what if we could find a way to infuse our daily lives with purpose, kindness, and discipline? What if we could cultivate a sense of inner cleanliness, not just for our bodies but for our very souls?

Here are three ways to exercise your soul, as inspired by William James:

1. Do someone a good turn and not get found out.

In a world where social media often dictates our every move, it's easy to get caught up in seeking validation and recognition. But what if we were to do a good deed, not for the sake of praise or reward, but simply because it brings us joy and fulfillment? This act of kindness can be as simple as holding the door for someone, offering a listening ear to a friend, or volunteering our time to a worthy cause. By doing good without the expectation of recognition, we can tap into a deeper sense of purpose and connection.

2. Do at least two things I don't want to do.

Let's face it – sobriety requires discipline and sacrifice. It's easy to get caught up in the comfort of our old habits and routines, but true growth and transformation often require us to step outside our comfort zones. By doing things we don't want to do, we can build resilience, develop new skills, and cultivate a sense of accomplishment. Whether it's attending a 12-step meeting, taking a challenging class, or simply getting out of bed earlier than usual, these small acts of discipline can have a profound impact on our sense of self and our journey toward sobriety.

3. Take action toward a goal that aligns with my values and principles.

As we work towards sobriety, it's essential to stay focused on our goals and values. What are the things that truly matter to us? What kind of person do we want to become? By taking action towards a goal that aligns with our values and principles, we can create a sense of direction and purpose. Whether it's setting small, achievable goals or working towards a larger vision, this sense of direction can help us stay motivated and inspired on our journey towards a cleaner, healthier soul.

As I reflect on these three ways to exercise my soul, I am reminded of the power of intentional living. By incorporating these practices into our daily lives, we can cultivate a sense of inner cleanliness, purpose, and fulfillment. We can become the kind of people who inspire others, who live with integrity, and who radiate a sense of joy and compassion.

So, I invite you to join me on this journey. Let's exercise our souls, one day at a time, and discover the transformative power of kindness, discipline, and purpose.

The Phoenix Rises

I was a master of chaos, a virtuoso of vice. My life was a never-ending cycle of booze, broads, and bad decisions. I thought I was invincible, that I could outrun the demons that haunted me. But the truth was, I was drowning in a sea of self-destruction.

My friends and family had given up on me, and I couldn't blame them. I was a shell of the person I once was, a shadow of my former self. The only thing that brought me fleeting joy was the next drink, the next high, the next conquest.

But the more I drank, the more I lost myself. The more I used it, the more I lost control. And the more I slept around, the more I lost respect for myself.

It was a vicious cycle, and I was trapped in it until the day I hit rock bottom.

I woke up in a hospital bed, my head pounding and my body aching. I had no idea how I got there or what had happened the night before. But as the fog lifted, I saw the devastation around me: the broken glass, the shattered dreams, the shattered lives.

That's when I knew I had to change. I had to face the music, to confront the demons that had been haunting me for so long. I checked myself into a treatment center, and for the first time in my life, I began to confront the truth.

The truth was, I was a broken man. I was a slave to my addictions, a prisoner of my own making. But I was also a survivor. I was a fighter. And I was determined to rise from the ashes like the phoenix.

The journey was tough, but I was determined to see it through. I attended therapy sessions, support groups, and counseling. I learned to confront my demons, face my fears, and let go of my past.

And slowly but surely, I began to heal. I began to see the world in a new light. I began to see myself in a new light. I began to see that I was more than just a drunk, more than just a user, more than just a womanizer.

I was a human being, worthy of love, worthy of respect, worthy of redemption.

Today, I am a recovering addict. I am a work in progress, but I am making progress. I am learning to live with purpose, to live with intention, and to live with integrity.

And I am grateful. I am grateful for the journey, for the struggles, for the setbacks. I am grateful for the people who supported me, who believed in me, and who loved me.

And I am grateful for the phoenix that rose from the ashes. I am grateful for the new me, the better me, the stronger me.

I am a work of art, a masterpiece in progress. And I am proud to be a recovering addict, proud to be a survivor, proud to be a phoenix rising from the ashes.

The Wiz Analogy

As I stepped out of the New River Treatment Center, I felt a sense of liberation wash over me. After 30 long years of battling alcoholism, I was finally taking control of my life. The journey had been tough, but the lessons I learned along the way would stay with me forever.

As I reflect on my experience, I am reminded of the Wiz characters who joined me on this journey.

Dorothy, the schoolteacher, was struggling with depression and anxiety issues, just like I was. She had lost her way, feeling stuck and helpless. But with the help of the treatment center, she discovered her inner strength and learned to cope with her emotions in a healthy way.

The Scarecrow, who had also struggled with alcoholism, joined Dorothy on her journey. He had been searching for a brain, but what he found was a newfound sense of purpose and direction. He learned that he didn't need a brain to be smart; rather, he needed to trust his instincts and make wise decisions.

The Tin Man, the amusement park leader, was struggling with womanizing and alcohol addiction. He had lost touch with his emotions and was feeling empty and hollow. But with the help of the treatment center, he discovered his heart and learned to connect with others on a deeper level.

And then there was the Lion, who struggled with courage and alcoholism. He had been afraid to take risks and face his fears, but with the help of the treatment center, he discovered his inner strength and learned to face his demons head-on.

As I look back on my journey, I realize that the lessons I learned from the Wiz characters are the same lessons I learned in treatment. I learned that:

* I don't have to be controlled by my emotions; rather, I can learn to manage them in a healthy way.

* I don't need a brain to be smart; rather, I can trust my instincts and make wise decisions.

* I don't have to be defined by my past; rather, I can learn to connect with others and find my true purpose.

* I don't have to be afraid to take risks and face my fears; rather, I can discover my inner strength and overcome my addiction.

As I walk away from the treatment center, I am filled with a sense of hope and excitement for the future. I know that I still have a long way to go, but I am confident that I have the tools and the support to overcome my addiction and live a fulfilling life.

To anyone who is struggling with addiction, I want to say that there is hope. There is a way out of the darkness and into the light. Don't be afraid to seek help, and don't be afraid to face your demons head-on. You are stronger than you think, and you are capable of overcoming anything.

As I look back on my journey, I am reminded of the words of the Wiz: "You've had the power all along, my dear." I may have thought that I was powerless against my addiction, but in reality, I had the power to overcome it all along. I just needed to believe in myself and take the first step toward recovery.

And so, I take that first step, and I continue on my journey towards a life of freedom and fulfillment. I am no longer controlled by my addiction; rather, I am in control of my life. I am Dorothy, the Scarecrow, the Tin Man, and the Lion, all rolled into one. I am a survivor, and I am a warrior. I am a work in progress, but I am proud of the progress I have made so far.

And as I walk away from the treatment center, I am filled with a sense of gratitude and appreciation for the journey I have been on. I am grateful for the lessons I learned, and I am grateful for the support I received along the way. I am grateful for the Wiz, who showed me that I had the power all along.

And as I look to the future, I am excited to see what lies ahead. I know that I will face challenges and setbacks along the way, but I am confident that I have the tools and the support to overcome them. I am confident that I will continue to grow and learn, and that I will continue to overcome my addiction.

And so, I take one final look at the treatment center, and I say goodbye. I am ready to take on the world, and I am ready to live a life of freedom and fulfillment. I am no longer controlled by my addiction; rather, I am in control of my life. I am a survivor, and I am a warrior. I am a work in progress, but I am proud of the progress I have made so far.

And as I walk away from the treatment center, I am filled with a sense of hope and excitement for the future. I know that I still have a long way to go, but I am confident that I have the tools and the support to overcome my addiction and live a fulfilling life.

The Power of Belief: Unlocking the Key to Overcoming Addiction

Belief is a powerful force that can either empower or cripple us. When it comes to overcoming addiction, the power of belief can be the difference between success and failure. In this chapter, we will delve into the importance of belief in conquering addiction and explore how to cultivate a strong belief in oneself and one's ability to overcome addiction.

Belief is the foundation upon which our thoughts, emotions, and actions are built. When we believe in ourselves and our abilities, we are more likely to take risks, push through challenges, and persevere in the face of adversity. On the other hand, when we lack belief in ourselves, we may become discouraged, give up easily, and struggle to make progress.

In the context of addiction, belief plays a crucial role in recovery. When individuals believe that they can overcome their addiction, they are more likely to stay committed to their treatment plan, attend therapy sessions, and make healthy lifestyle choices. Conversely, when individuals lack belief in their ability to recover, they may become disheartened, relapse, and struggle to make progress.

So, how can we cultivate a strong belief in ourselves and our ability to overcome addiction? The answer lies in developing a growth mindset, focusing on our strengths, and reframing negative thoughts. By adopting a growth mindset, we can view challenges as opportunities for growth and development rather than threats to our ego. By focusing on our strengths, we can build confidence and self-esteem, which can help us stay motivated and committed to our recovery. And by reframing negative thoughts, we can replace self-doubt and fear with positive and empowering beliefs.

The power of belief is a powerful tool in overcoming addiction. By cultivating a strong belief in ourselves and our ability to recover, we can stay motivated, committed, and empowered to achieve our goals. Remember, belief is not just a feeling; it's a choice. Choose to believe in yourself and your ability to overcome addiction, and you will be amazed at the progress you can make.

The Magic of Mindfulness: A Powerful Tool for Overcoming Addiction

As we navigate the complexities of life, it's easy to get caught up in the whirlwind of emotions, thoughts, and distractions. But what if I told you that there's a way to break free from this cycle and tap into a deeper sense of calm and clarity? Enter the magic of mindfulness.

For those who have struggled with addiction, the journey to recovery can be a long and arduous one. But what if I told you that mindfulness can be a game changer? By cultivating a sense of awareness and presence, you can begin to let go of the past, quiet the mind, and find peace in the present.

As someone who has personally struggled with addiction, I can attest to the transformative power of mindfulness. In my darkest moments, I felt lost and alone, unable to escape the grip of my demons. But through the practice of mindfulness, I discovered a sense of calm and clarity that I had never known before.

So, how does it work? Mindfulness is simply the practice of paying attention to the present moment, without judgment or distraction. It's about acknowledging your thoughts, emotions, and physical sensations without getting caught up in them. By doing so, you can begin to break free from the cycle of addiction and cultivate a sense of inner peace.

But don't just take my word for it. Research has shown that mindfulness can be a powerful tool in the recovery process. Studies have found that mindfulness can reduce symptoms of anxiety and depression, improve emotional regulation, and even decrease cravings for addictive substances.

So, how can you start practicing mindfulness? It's simpler than you might think. Start by taking a few deep breaths, focusing on the sensation of the air moving in and out of your body. Then, bring your attention to the present moment, noticing the sights, sounds, and sensations around you.

As you continue to practice, you'll begin to notice subtle changes in your thoughts, emotions, and physical sensations. You'll feel more grounded, more centered, and more at peace. And as you do, you'll find that you're better equipped to handle the challenges of recovery and to stay on the path to a healthier, happier you.

So, if you're struggling with addiction, I urge you to give mindfulness a try. It may just be the magic you need to overcome your demons and find peace in the present.

Self Expert

I'm not sure where to begin, as the journey of self-discovery has been a long and arduous one. My life has been a tangled web of addictions, abandonment, anxiety, and ADHD. It's a wonder I'm still standing, to be honest.

For years, I wore a mask of confidence and charm, hiding behind a facade of womanizing and substance abuse. I was a charlatan, a master of deception, and a puzzle to myself. I was tired of being a mystery, tired of living a lie. But the truth was, I was drowning in my own despair.

The treatment center was a turning point for me. It was a place where I could finally confront the demons that had haunted me for so long: the darkness that had consumed me and the emptiness that had left me feeling hollow. It was a place where I could finally face the truth about myself.

As I sat in those therapy sessions, I began to unravel the tangled threads of my past. I began to see the patterns, the cycles of abuse and abandonment that had shaped me into the person I was today. I began to understand the root causes of my addictions, my anxiety, and my ADHD.

It was a painful process, to say the least. There were times when I felt like I was reliving every painful moment of my past, every hurt and every betrayal. But it was also a liberating experience. For the first time in my life, I felt like I was taking control, like I was finally facing the truth about myself.

I learned that my addictions were a cry for help, a desperate attempt to fill the void that had been left in me. I learned that my womanizing was a way to avoid intimacy, to avoid getting too close to anyone. And I learned that my substance abuse was a way to numb the pain, to escape the reality of my situation.

But most importantly, I learned that I was not alone. I learned that I was not a monster, that I was not a bad person. I learned that I was a human being, flawed and imperfect, but worthy of love and compassion.

The treatment center was a place of healing, a place of transformation. It was a place where I could finally let go of the past, where I could finally start to rebuild myself. It was a place where I could finally find peace and solace.

As I look back on my journey, I am reminded of the power of vulnerability and the power of honesty. I am reminded that it's okay to be broken and that it's okay to be imperfect. I am also reminded that it's never too late to start anew and to start again.

I am still on this journey, still learning and growing. But I am no longer the same person I was before. I am no longer the charlatan, the enigma. I am no longer the addict, the womanizer. I am no longer the person I used to be.

I am someone new, someone different. I am someone who is finally facing the truth about themselves, someone who is finally taking control of their life. And I am someone who is finally finding peace, finally finding solace.

The Four Horsemen

I still remember the darkest days of my life, consumed by the demons of addiction, anxiety, and abandonment. I was a master of disguise, a chameleon who could blend in with the crowd, but beneath the surface, I was a tangled mess of insecurities and self-destructive tendencies. My womanizing and excessive drinking had become a toxic habit, a desperate attempt to fill the void within.

But then, something changed. I stumbled upon a treatment center that promised a new beginning —a chance to break free from the shackles of my addictions. It was there, during the quiet hours of my recovery, that I discovered a book that would change my life forever: "The Four Agreements" by Don Miguel Ruiz.

The words of the book were like a balm for my soul, a gentle reminder that I didn't have to be a slave to my emotions andthat I could choose to live differently. The first agreement, "Be Impeccable with Your Word," resonated deeply with me. I realized that my words, actions, and intentions had reflected my inner turmoil. I had been living a lie, pretending to be someone I wasn't, and it was time to take responsibility for my words and actions.

The second agreement, "Don't Take Anything Personally," was a transformative experience for me. I had always been sensitive to the opinions of others, and my self-worth had been closely tied to their validation. However, as I read those words, I realized that I didn't have to carry the burdens of others. I could choose to release the need for approval and concentrate on my own inner truth.

The third agreement, "Don't Make Assumptions," was difficult for me to accept. I had always been inclined to jump to conclusions, making assumptions about both others and myself. However, as I read those words, I recognized that assumptions are a recipe for disaster, a means of constructing a reality that is not grounded in facts. I needed to learn to ask questions, seek clarity, and trust that the truth would eventually reveal itself.

The fourth agreement, "Always Do Your Best," served as a reminder that I didn't need to be perfect. I didn't have to pretend to be someone I wasn't. I simply needed to show up, be present, and give my best effort. This realization brought a liberating sense of freedom from the weight of expectation.

As I read those words, I felt a weight lift off my shoulders. A sense of peace, clarity, and purpose washed over me. I realized that I didn't have to be a slave to my addictions; I could choose to live a life of integrity, authenticity, and purpose.

The Four Agreements became my guiding principles, my North Star, and my beacon of hope. They helped me navigate the treacherous waters of recovery, find my footing, and build a life that was true to my authentic self.

I am not the same person I once was. While I am still a work in progress, I am no longer the enigma, the charlatan, the womanizer, or the drunkard. I am a man who is learning to live with integrity, to be true to himself, and to discover purpose in his life.

And it is all thanks to the Four Agreements.

The Dreamer

"A Dreamer" - a man who defied the odds, rising above the turbulent waters of anxiety, abandonment, and ADHD to emerge victorious in his journey toward recovery. His story is a testament to the human spirit's capacity for resilience and determination.

Born against all odds, "A Dreamer" confronted a life filled with uncertainty from the very beginning. His early years were characterized by anxiety, a constant companion that whispered doubts and fears in his ear. The burden of abandonment, coupled with a sense of being left behind, only intensified his struggles. To complicate matters further, ADHD—a condition that hindered his ability to focus and stay on track—added another layer of challenge to his life.

As he grew older, "A Dreamer" resorted to substance abuse as a way to cope with his emotional pain. It provided a temporary escape, a fleeting sense of relief from the turmoil that raged within him. However, like a siren's song, it continually beckoned him back, ensnaring him in a relentless cycle of addiction.

Yet, despite the odds stacked against him, "A Dreamer" refused to surrender. He understood that he was more than the sum of his struggles; he had a purpose to fulfill and a dream to pursue. With renewed determination, he embarked on the long and arduous journey of recovery.

It was not an easy journey, by any means. There were setbacks and relapses, as well as moments of despair and frustration. However, "A Dreamer" persevered, driven by his steadfast commitment to his own well-being. He sought help, support, and guidance, and gradually, he began to rebuild his life.

Today, "A Dreamer" serves as a testament to the resilience of the human spirit. His story is a beacon of hope, reminding us that no matter how dark the night may appear, there is always a path forward. He has learned to manage his anxiety, channel his ADHD into productive outlets, and find solace in the support of others.

But "A Dreamer's" greatest achievement is not his recovery; rather, it is the lessons he has learned along the way. He has discovered that true strength lies not in the absence of struggles, but in the ability to confront them head-on. He has learned that vulnerability is a strength, not a weakness, and that seeking help is a sign of courage, not defeat.

As we look to the future, it is important to remember the story of "A Dreamer". We must recognize that we are all "Dreamers" at heart, navigating a world that is often uncertain and unpredictable. Let us draw inspiration from his journey, find the strength to confront our own challenges, and never give up on our dreams.

Reflections

As I reflect on my life, I confront a complex tapestry of struggles, each thread intertwining to create a narrative of addiction, abandonment, anxiety, and ADHD. For years, I allowed these demons to define me, perpetuating a cycle of self-destruction that left me feeling lost and disconnected from the world.

My journey began with a pattern of womanizing and substance abuse, a desperate attempt to fill the void left by my feelings of abandonment. I became a charlatan, pretending to be someone I was not, and an enigma, hiding behind a facade of confidence and bravado. However, beneath the surface, I was drowning in a sea of despair, unable to escape the crushing weight of my insecurities.

It wasn't until I checked into a treatment center that I began to confront the true nature of my demons. In a safe and supportive environment, I was able to peel back the layers of my psyche, revealing the deep-seated fears and anxieties that had driven me to self-destructive behaviors. I was compelled to face the reality of my ADHD and how it had contributed to my addiction and impulsivity.

But it was in this darkness that I discovered a glimmer of hope. As I navigated my challenges, I began to see myself in a new light. I realized that I was not a victim of circumstance, but rather a survivor of my own making. I was not a charlatan;

I was a complex and multifaceted individual deserving of love and respect.

Today, I am proud to announce that I am in recovery. I have learned to manage my ADHD and channel my energy and creativity into positive outlets. I have formed meaningful connections with others and discovered a sense of purpose and direction that I never thought possible.

My journey has not been easy, and I have encountered numerous setbacks along the way. However, I have learned that it is during our darkest moments that we uncover the greatest opportunities for growth and transformation. I have come to understand that it is possible to rise above our demons, confront our fears and anxieties, and emerge stronger and more resilient on the other side.

As I reflect on my life, I am reminded that recovery is not a destination but a journey. It is a process of continuous growth and self-discovery, involving the navigation of the complexities of our minds and emotions. I am grateful to be on this journey, knowing that I am not alone and that there is always hope for a brighter tomorrow.

I am an Enigma

I am a riddle, a mystery shrouded in darkness. My existence was a relentless dance with the devil, a siren's song of self-destruction. I was a virtuoso of vice, a maestro of mayhem, and a conductor of chaos. My life was a symphony of alcohol, women, and poor choices—a cacophony of turmoil that echoed through the corridors of my mind.

I believed I was invincible, capable of outrunning the demons that haunted me. I thought I could tame the beast lurking within and contain the storm raging inside me. However, the truth was that I was drowning in a sea of self-destruction. The waves of whiskey and fleeting relationships crashed against the shores of my soul, eroding the fragile walls of my sanity.

I was a master of chaos, a weaver of webs spun with deceit and destruction. I was a chameleon, shifting colors to match the mood of the moment and adapting to the whims of my desires. I was a thief, seizing fleeting moments of pleasure from the grasp of fate, only to lose them in the sands of time.

But beneath the surface, beneath the bravado and bluster, I was a shipwreck—a sinking vessel of shattered dreams and broken promises. I was a ghost, haunting the corridors of my own mind, searching for a way out of the darkness that had engulfed me.

And yet, even as I was drowning, I found myself irresistibly drawn to the undertow of destruction. I was like a moth to a flame, a fly ensnared in a spider's web. I became a slave to my own desires, a prisoner of my own demons.

But the truth was, I was not invincible. I was neither a god nor a superhero; I was simply a man—a fragile, fallible human being—struggling to navigate my way through the darkness. Ultimately, it was not the demons that destroyed me, but rather my own hand, my own choices, and my own self-destruction.

I am a riddle, a mystery cloaked in darkness. I embody a narrative of chaos, destruction, self-destruction, and despair. Yet, I am also a tale of hope, redemption, the potential for forgiveness, and the promise of a new beginning.

The Burden of Stagnation

It's a feeling that settles deep within, like a heavy fog that refuses to lift. Yet, we often find ourselves trapped, unable to break free from the shackles of our own making. The reason, my friends, lies not in the circumstances that surround us, but in the very fabric of our character.

We rehearse the same victim day in and day out, wondering why we haven't made any progress.

We play the same roles, adopt the same personas, and expect different outcomes. The truth is, we are the authors of our own stories, and it's time we take responsibility for the script we are writing.

We've all experienced it—being stuck in a rut, feeling as though we're making no progress. We replay the same conversations, relive the same memories, and experience the same emotions, yet we anticipate a different outcome. We hope that familiar patterns will suddenly shift, that old habits will magically vanish, and that persistent emotions will abruptly fade away. However, this transformation will not occur until we confront the one obstacle that holds us back: ourselves.

We often replay the same victim narrative because we fear taking the leap, stepping out of our comfort zones, and risking failure. We are afraid to be vulnerable, to be seen, and to be heard. We fear embracing our true selves. Consequently, we hide behind the mask of victimhood, using it as an excuse to avoid the very experiences that could liberate us.

But freedom is not found in victimhood, my friends. Freedom is discovered through the courage to confront our fears, face our doubts, and rise above our limitations. It is found in the willingness to take leaps, embrace risks, and trust in ourselves.

So, I urge you, my friends, to stop rehearsing the same victim narrative. Stop playing the same roles, stop adopting the same personas, and stop expecting different outcomes. Take responsibility for your own story and write a new chapter—one of courage, resilience, and hope. Write a chapter that declares, "I am enough and "I am worthy."

Remember, you are the author of your own story. You have the power to shape what happens next. So, take the pen and start writing. Begin a new chapter—one that is filled with purpose, passion, and promise.

The Shackles of Victimhood

How often do individuals find themselves trapped in a cycle of suffering, repeatedly encountering the same situations and reliving identical narratives? It seems as though one is ensnared in an endless loop, enduring the same pain, betrayal, and disillusionment. Amidst this turmoil, individuals frequently overlook the chance to rewrite their own stories.

Substance abuse became the predominant adversary in my life. It evolved into a constant companion, a trusted confidant, and a reliable means of escape. However, when I looked into the mirror, I was met by a stranger—a figure that seemed lost, broken, and defeated. In this situation, I found myself playing the role of the victim instead of embracing my true self.

It is essential to recognize that progress cannot be achieved without addressing the underlying issues that hinder our advancement. Liberation from the constraints of addiction requires acknowledging the emotional distress that drives individuals to seek solace in substances. This process does not focus on assigning blame to oneself or others; instead, it highlights the importance of taking responsibility for one's own life narrative.

The process of overcoming substance abuse in my life proved to be a formidable challenge. It was a daily struggle, an ongoing conflict, and an internal battle. However, as time passed, I began to view myself from a new perspective. I started to recognize my strength, resilience, and character. I came to the realization that I was not a victim, but rather a warrior.

As I emerged from the grips of addiction, I uncovered a transformative narrative defined by hope, redemption, and triumph. I gained the ability to reframe the story of my life, assert control over my circumstances, and shape my own future. With each progressive step, I experienced a gradual alleviation of the burdens of my past, akin to the dawn breaking over the horizon.

To anyone still caught in the cycle of addiction, I want to convey this: You are not a victim; you are a warrior. You are strong, capable, and deserving of a life free from the shackles of substance abuse. Reclaim your narrative, rewrite your story, and choose your own destiny. You are worthy of a fulfilling, rich, and meaningful life.

Remember, sometimes the reason we haven't progressed is that we cling to a victim mentality rather than embracing our true character. However, it is never too late to rewrite our narrative, take control of our lives, and choose our own destiny.

Calmness

The cacophony of thoughts swirling within our minds presents a constant struggle to make sense of the chaos surrounding us. It feels as though we are adrift in a sea of faces, desperately searching for a lifeline to guide us back to our true selves. Yet, in this era of social media, where everyone seems to be a guru, thought leader, or influencer, it is all too easy to be swept away by the tide of conformity.

We are constantly bombarded with messages dictating who we should be, what we should wear, what we should eat, and what we should believe. The noise is overwhelming, and it's no wonder we often feel lost, uncertain, and disconnected from our true identities. In our pursuit of fitting in, gaining approval, and seeking acceptance, we frequently neglect to listen to our inner voices, trust our instincts, and honor our unique experiences.

But what if we could find a way to quiet the noise of external expectations and tune into our own inner wisdom? What if we could pinpoint the true north of our souls and navigate a path that is authentic, meaningful, and fulfilling? This is where the power of community becomes vital. We need individuals who can help us recognize our true selves amidst a sea of followers, who can mirror our strengths, weaknesses, and passions back to us.

For me, sobriety has been a journey of self-discovery, unraveling the threads of my identity from the intricate web of addiction. It has involved peeling back layers, confronting my fears, and embracing my vulnerability. This journey has also necessitated surrounding myself with individuals who can genuinely see, hear, and support me along this path.

These individuals can help us identify our position within a crowd of followers, reflecting our unique light back to us and guiding us toward our true selves. They assist us in silencing the noise and attuning to our inner wisdom. They are the ones who can help us navigate our journey, even when the path ahead is unclear.

Let us not hesitate to seek out individuals who can help us discover our true selves amidst a crowd of followers. We should embrace vulnerability, authenticity, and the freedom to be ourselves. Ultimately, it is not about conforming, seeking approval, or gaining acceptance; it is about remaining true to ourselves and leading a life that is genuine, meaningful, and fulfilling.

Unapologetically You

As I sit here reflecting on my journey of recovery from substance abuse, I am reminded of the power of authenticity. There is no substitute for being genuine about who you are, what you stand for, and how you respond when the storms of life come crashing down.

My journey began with a profound sense of desperation. I found myself ensnared in a cycle of addiction, feeling lost and isolated, with no clear direction or purpose. However, as I sought help and support, I came to understand that the only path to genuine healing was through honesty—both with myself and with others. I had to confront the demons that had been holding me back, and I needed to do so with courage and vulnerability.

It wasn't easy. There were moments when I felt like giving up, when the pain and shame seemed unbearable. However, I refused to let my struggles define me. I chose to confront my fears directly and challenge the lies and misconceptions that had been holding me back. As I did, I began to experience a sense of freedom and empowerment that I had never felt before.

Being genuine with myself and others was the key to my recovery. It enabled me to shed the masks and pretenses that had concealed my true self. This authenticity allowed me to be vulnerable and to openly share my struggles and fears. As a result, I was able to connect with others on a deeper level, forming meaningful relationships grounded in trust and understanding.

As I reflect on my journey, I am reminded of the significance of authenticity. It serves as the foundation upon which all genuine relationships are built. Authenticity is the key to healing and personal growth, enabling us to overcome adversity and reach our full potential. Moreover, it is the only way to truly live and to be ourselves amidst life's challenges.

I want to encourage anyone who is struggling with addiction or any other challenge to be genuine with themselves and others. Don't be afraid to be vulnerable; embrace openness and honesty about your struggles and fears. Allow your true self to shine through. When you do, you will discover that you are capable of overcoming even the greatest challenges, emerging stronger, wiser, and more resilient than ever before.

As I embark on this journey of recovery from substance abuse, I am reminded of the importance of being true to myself, understanding my values, and maintaining my integrity when faced with life's challenges. It may be a cliché, but it holds true—authenticity is essential for overcoming any obstacle, including addiction.

For far too long, I allowed my struggles with substance abuse to define my identity. I concealed my true feelings behind a facade of confidence and bravado, pretending that everything was fine when, in reality, I was submerged in a sea of self-doubt and fear. The truth is, I was never truly okay. I felt lost, alone, and terrified.

But today, I am choosing to be authentic. I am opting for vulnerability, honesty, and embracing my true self—flaws and all. It's not easy, but it is essential. When life's storms arrive—and they inevitably will—I want to stand tall and declare, "I am enough."

Recovery is not merely about abstaining from substances; it is about becoming the best version of yourself. It involves learning to love and accept yourself, flaws and all. It is about discovering your purpose and passion and pursuing them with unwavering determination.

As I navigate this journey, I am reminded of the strength of community. I am surrounded by individuals who believe in me, support me, and encourage me to become my best self, for which I am truly grateful.

But I am also reminded of the importance of self-care. Recovery is not solely about achieving sobriety; it encompasses nurturing your mind, body, and spirit. It involves discovering healthy methods to manage stress and anxiety, as well as prioritizing your overall well-being.

As I look to the future, I am filled with anticipation for what lies ahead. I am eager to continue growing, learning, and evolving into the best version of myself. Additionally, I look forward to sharing my journey with others, hoping to inspire and motivate them to embark on their own paths of self-improvement.

So, to anyone who is struggling with addiction, I want you to know that you are not alone. You are strong, capable, and deserving of a life free from the chains of substance abuse. To those on the journey of recovery, remember that you are doing your best, and that is something to be proud of.

Remember, being authentic about who you are, what you stand for, and how you respond when life's storms arise is essential for overcoming any obstacle. Therefore, be courageous, be open, and be true to yourself. The world needs more of this.

Celebrate the small victories.

As I stand at the threshold of a new day, I am filled with a sense of determination and resilience. The weight of my past struggles still lingers, but I am no longer defined by them. I am a warrior—scarred yet stronger—armed with a renewed sense of purpose.

Recovery is not a destination; it is a journey. It consists of a series of small victories, setbacks, and personal growth. It requires a continual re-evaluation of my current position and my aspirations. Today, I am choosing to refocus, reset, and reaffirm my commitment to my vision.

I reflect on the darkest days when the world appeared to move in slow motion, and I felt as though I were trapped in quicksand. However, I refused to give up. I would not allow the shadows to consume me. I fought back with every fiber of my being, and gradually, I began to emerge from the darkness.

Today, I take pride in the progress I have made. I am proud of the person I am becoming, the strength I have discovered within myself, and the valuable lessons I have learned along the way.

But I understand that recovery is not a one-time achievement; it is an ongoing process, a daily choice to continue moving forward, to persevere through challenging times, and to maintain belief in myself. Therefore, I choose to refocus on my vision, reset my priorities, and reaffirm my commitment to my goals.

I am not the same person I was yesterday, nor the person I was the day before or the week prior. I am evolving, growing, and changing. I am eager to see where this journey takes me and to discover the person I will become and the accomplishments I will achieve.

So, as I embark on this new day, I am filled with hope and anticipation. I am prepared to confront whatever challenges arise, equipped with the understanding that I am strong, capable, and resilient. I am ready to take another step toward my vision, moving closer to the person I am destined to become.

As I look to the future, I am reminded that each day presents a new opportunity to begin anew, to refocus, to reset, and to reaffirm my goals. Every day is a chance to move closer to my vision and to my authentic self. I am eager to see what the future has in store.

Dealing with Substance Abuse: Divorcing the Inner Enemy

The War Within It's a battle we all face, yet few acknowledge. The enemy lies not outside, but within. It manifests as the voices in our heads, the thoughts that haunt us, and the demons we have invited into our lives. For many, substance abuse serves as a coping mechanism—a temporary escape from the pain and chaos. However, it creates a vicious cycle, a relentless struggle that consumes us, leaving us broken and defeated.

The truth is, our greatest enemy is not the bottle, the pill, or the pipe. It is the thoughts we cling to, the past we cannot release, and the fears that ensnare us. It is the "inner me that whispers lies, fuels our insecurities, and prevents us from achieving greatness.

We've all experienced it. We've all felt the sting of rejection, the burden of shame, and the devastating impact of failure. However, it is in those moments that we face a choice. We can allow the adversary to triumph, or we can rise up and reclaim our power.

Divorcing the inner self is not an easy task. It is a painful process, a journey of self-discovery, and a struggle for our very souls. However, it is the only way to break free from the chains that bind us. It is the only way to silence the voices that whisper lies and to find the strength to overcome.

So, how do we achieve this? How do we separate from our inner selves and regain control? It begins with awareness. We must acknowledge the adversary within—the thoughts that hinder us and the fears that constrain us. We need to recognize that our greatest enemy is not the external world, but our own minds.

Next, we must confront our adversary. We must face our fears, insecurities, and shame. We need to acknowledge the pain and hurt, and we must release the burdens of the past. It is essential to learn to forgive ourselves and others, and we must consciously choose to let go of anger and resentment.

Finally, we must replace the negative narrative with a new, empowering one. We should fill our minds with positive thoughts, affirmations of our self-worth, and a strong sense of purpose. It is essential to surround ourselves with uplifting and supportive individuals, and to discover healthy coping mechanisms to manage stress and anxiety.

Dealing with substance abuse is not easy. It is a lifelong journey, a daily battle, and a constant struggle. However, it is worth it. It is worth it to be free, to be whole, and to become the best version of ourselves. So, let us rise up and reclaim control. Let's divorce the inner me and discover our true selves.

Discover Your Garden

As I reflect on my journey of self-discovery and personal growth, I have come to understand that making mistakes early on was essential to becoming the person I am today. It is a difficult truth, but one that I have learned to accept and even celebrate.

In the past, I was often hesitant to take risks and make mistakes. I believed that doing so would lead to judgment, criticism, or, worse, failure. However, as I reflect on those times, I realize that those fears were preventing me from truly living and becoming the best version of myself.

It wasn't until I began to embrace my mistakes and view them as opportunities for growth that I truly started to flourish. I learned to see failure as a stepping stone to success rather than a reason to give up. With each mistake, I became more resilient, adaptable, and confident.

I've come to understand that making mistakes early on is not a sign of weakness, but rather a demonstration of courage. It takes considerable bravery to take risks and put yourself out there, even if it means confronting the possibility of failure. It is in those moments of vulnerability that we truly learn and grow.

As I reflect on my journey, I am reminded of the numerous times I have made mistakes and learned valuable lessons from them. I have developed greater patience, empathy, and compassion. I have also learned to trust myself and my abilities, even in the face of uncertainty.

Most importantly, I have learned to forgive both myself and others. I understand that everyone makes mistakes, and what truly matters is how we respond to them. By embracing our errors and viewing them as opportunities for growth, we can become the best versions of ourselves and lead lives filled with purpose and fulfillment. Making mistakes early on should not be a source of shame; rather, it should be celebrated. It signifies courage, resilience, and a willingness to learn and grow. As I continue my journey of self-discovery and personal development, I am reminded that it is perfectly acceptable to make mistakes, as long as I am committed to learning from them and striving to become a better version of myself.

Dealing with Substance Abuse: A Journey Toward Redemption

The pity party is over, and it's time to uninvite the guest of honor—you. It's time to take control of your life and break free from the chains of substance abuse. The journey to redemption is challenging, but it is a vital step toward healing and recovery.

Substance abuse is a thief that robs you of your identity, relationships, and sense of self-worth. It is a master manipulator that convinces you that you are not good enough and that you need it to feel complete. However, the truth is that you are enough, and you do not need it to be happy.

The first step toward recovery is acknowledging that you have a problem. This involves admitting that you are powerless over your addiction and that your life has become unmanageable. Although this step can be challenging, it is essential. Once you have recognized your problem, you can begin working toward a solution.

The next step is to seek help. This assistance can take various forms, including therapy, support groups, or rehabilitation programs. It is essential to find a support system that meets your needs and with which you feel comfortable. Having a team of individuals who understand your experiences can significantly impact your recovery journey.

Another important step is self-care, which encompasses attending to your physical, emotional, and spiritual well-being. This can include activities such as exercise, meditation, and spending time in nature. Furthermore, it is essential to surround yourself with positive individuals who support your recovery.

Redemption is achievable, but it demands hard work and commitment. It is a journey filled with challenges, yet it is one that is worthwhile to pursue. You possess the strength to conquer your addiction and lead a fulfilling, healthy life.

So, don't give up. Keep pushing forward, even when it feels as though the world is against you. You have the strength to overcome your addiction, and you deserve a happy, healthy life.

Go Make It Happen

There are certain aspects of life that only you can handle. No matter how much you attempt to delegate or outsource, some tasks demand your personal touch and effort. These are the elements that define you and distinguish you from others.

Think about it: have you ever seen an advertisement that says, "Lease a Dieter" or "Rent a Runner"? No, because those pursuits cannot be outsourced or delegated. Losing weight and getting fit require dedication, discipline, and hard work. You cannot hire someone to do it for you, regardless of how much money you possess.

The same principle applies to building strong relationships, achieving your goals, and pursuing your passions. These endeavors demand your time, effort, and energy. You cannot delegate them to someone else, regardless of their skills or experience.

But here's the reality: when you take ownership of your responsibilities, invest effort, and make sacrifices, the rewards are immeasurable. You will experience a profound sense of pride and accomplishment that cannot be derived from anyone else. You will be able to look in the mirror and say, "I did this. I achieved this."

So, don't be afraid to tackle the challenges that no one else can face for you. Embrace the hard work and make the necessary sacrifices. When you do, you'll be astonished by what you can accomplish and the person you can become.

Remember, no one else can do it for you, but you have the power to do it for yourself. You can take control of your life, your goals, and your dreams. You have the ability to make it happen. So, go out there and turn your aspirations into reality.

One Shining Moment

This very moment, I will change my life. It is a declaration that resonates through the corridors of my mind, serving as a beacon of hope and empowerment. The truth is, there has never been a moment, nor will there ever be, when I lack the power to alter my destiny.

In this moment, I am reminded that every decision, action, and thought has the potential to shape the course of my life. The choices I make, the words I speak, and the actions I take all possess the power to create a ripple effect that can either propel me forward or hold me back.

The beauty of this realization lies in understanding that it is not about waiting for a mythical "perfect" moment to arrive. It is not about waiting for circumstances to align or for external factors to fall into place. Rather, it is about recognizing that I have the power to create my own destiny, right here and right now.

This moment represents a turning point, a crossroads where I can choose to take control of my life and steer it in the direction I desire. It is an opportunity to break free from the shackles of fear, doubt, and uncertainty, and to take the driver's seat of my own destiny.

So, I choose to seize this moment. I choose to take a deep breath, focus on my goals, and take deliberate action to make them a reality. I choose to silence the voices of self-doubt and amplify the whispers of encouragement that reside within me.

At this moment, I am reminded that I am the architect of my own life and the master of my own destiny. With this knowledge, I feel empowered to create a life that is authentic, meaningful, and fulfilling.

So, I will change my life today. I will take the first step, followed by the next, and then the one after that. I will persevere through the obstacles, and I will celebrate each victory. As I do this, I will recognize that I am living the life I was meant to lead, and that I hold the power to make it a reality.

"I Shall Have What I Say"

The power of declaration is a formidable force that can shape our destiny. When we articulate our intentions, we awaken a profound sense of purpose and determination within ourselves. Today, I choose to declare my intentions boldly and unequivocally: I will achieve what I affirm. I will become the person that God created and intended me to be.

For too long, I have allowed doubts and fears to whisper in my ear, convincing me that my dreams are mere fantasies—unattainable and unrealistic. But no more. I have come to realize that my thoughts and words possess the power to shape my reality. I have been dreaming about my future, but now it is time to transform those dreams into reality.

I will embrace the person God created me to be, utilizing all my unique talents, gifts, and passions. I will become the leader, innovator, and change-maker I am destined to be. I will strive to make a difference in the world, leaving a lasting impact on those around me.

No longer will I allow fear to hold me back. No longer will I settle for mediocrity. I will be bold, I will be fearless, I will be unstoppable. I will be the master of my own destiny, shaping my future with purpose and intention.

I will attain what I declare because I have faith in myself. I trust in my abilities, my strengths, and my resilience. I am confident that I can achieve greatness, overcome any obstacle, and realize my wildest dreams.

So I declare: I will have what I say. I will be who God created and intended me to be. No longer will I merely dream about it; it shall come to pass.

Rumi's Poem

As I sat in the treatment center, enveloped by the familiar scent of antiseptic and the hum of fluorescent lights, I discovered a poem that would alter the course of my journey. Rumi's words, "Yesterday I was clever, so I wanted to change the world. Today I am wise, so I am changing myself," resonated profoundly within me. It felt as though the poet was speaking directly to my soul.

I have always been driven by a desire to change the world. I wanted to make a difference and leave a lasting impact. However, my aspirations for greatness were often overshadowed by my personal demons. My substance abuse had become a crutch, a means to numb the pain and distract myself from the emptiness within. I was intelligent, indeed, but my intelligence was merely a facade, a thin veil concealing the truth of my own brokenness.

But as I read Rumi's poem, something shifted within me. I realized that I had been attempting to change the world out of fear of confronting my own flaws. I was afraid to admit that I was not perfect, that I was struggling, and that I was broken. However, Rumi's words conveyed a different kind of wisdom. They emphasized the importance of self-awareness and the necessity of acknowledging our own limitations and imperfections.

As I delved deeper into my recovery, I began to understand that true change starts from within. It begins with acknowledging our flaws and weaknesses and working to overcome them. It involves being honest with ourselves, admitting that we are not perfect and that we need help. It requires being kind to ourselves, treating ourselves with the same compassion and understanding that we would extend to a friend.

Rumi's poem became a guiding light for me, reminding me that true wisdom lies not in attempting to change the world, but in transforming ourselves. It involves acknowledging our own brokenness and working towards healing it. It requires being gentle with ourselves and treating ourselves with kindness and compassion.

As I reflect on my journey, I am reminded of the profound wisdom in Rumi's words. They convey a unique understanding, one grounded in self-awareness and self-acceptance. They remind me that true transformation begins from within, and that the most impactful action I can take is to change myself.

Confucius Quote

As I reflect on my time at the treatment center, I am reminded of the profound lessons I learned about resilience, perseverance, and the strength of the human spirit. The journey was not easy, but it has left an indelible mark on my life.

One of the most significant takeaways was the understanding that failure is an inevitable part of growth. While this concept can be daunting, it serves as a reminder that we are not defined by our mistakes. Instead, it is our response to these failures that truly matters. As Confucius so eloquently stated, "A man is great not because he hasn't failed; a man is great because failure hasn't stopped him."

During my time at the treatment center, I encountered numerous challenges and setbacks. There were moments of frustration, anger, and despair; however, it was during those darkest times that I discovered my inner strength. I learned to confront my fears, face my demons, and rise above the ashes of my failures.

The treatment center offered a safe and supportive environment where I could confront my challenges directly. The therapists, counselors, and peers were all exceptionally knowledgeable and compassionate, providing guidance and encouragement at every step. They assisted me in identifying the root causes of my difficulties, developing coping mechanisms, and fostering a sense of self-worth.

One of the most powerful tools I have learned is the concept of mindfulness. By focusing on the present moment, I have been able to let go of the past and stop worrying about the future. I have learned to breathe, meditate, and practice self-compassion. These skills have proven invaluable in my daily life, helping me remain grounded and centered even in the face of adversity.

Another important lesson I learned was the significance of community. I was surrounded by individuals who understood my struggles, had faced similar challenges, and were dedicated to supporting one another. We formed strong bonds by sharing our stories, fears, and hopes. We uplifted each other, offering words of encouragement and celebrating one another's successes.

As I reflect on my time at the treatment center, I am filled with a profound sense of gratitude and admiration. I am thankful for the lessons I learned, the friendships I forged, and the support I received. I am also in awe of the resilience of the human spirit, which can triumph over even the most formidable challenges.

My time at the treatment center was a transformative experience that taught me invaluable lessons about resilience, perseverance, and the strength of the human spirit. Although the journey was challenging, it ultimately left me stronger, wiser, and more compassionate. As I move forward, I am reminded that failure is an inevitable aspect of growth; however, it is our response to it that truly matters.

Marcus Aurelius Quote

As I reflect on my journey through the treatment center, I am reminded of the profound wisdom of Marcus Aurelius: "The nearer a man comes to a calm mind, the closer he is to strength." These words resonate deeply with me, as I struggled to find peace and serenity amidst the turmoil of my addiction.

Upon entering the treatment center, I was overwhelmed by a sense of uncertainty and fear. The prospect of confronting my demons and facing the harsh reality of my addiction felt daunting. However, as I began to engage with the program, I started to understand that the journey was not about evading the pain, but about embracing it.

Through the guidance of my therapists and the support of my peers, I learned to confront my emotions and thoughts directly. I discovered that the more I attempted to suppress my feelings, the more they overwhelmed me. However, by acknowledging and accepting them, I began to experience a sense of liberation.

One of the most significant lessons I learned was the importance of self-compassion. I realized that I had been overly critical of myself, dwelling on every mistake and perceived failure. However, as I began to practice self-compassion, I started to view myself in a new light. I learned to be kind and understanding toward myself, just as I would be toward a close friend.

Another crucial aspect of my journey was the development of mindfulness. I learned to focus on the present moment rather than dwelling on the past or worrying about the future. This practice allowed me to cultivate a sense of calm and clarity, even amidst chaos.

As I progressed through the program, I began to realize that the journey was not solely about me. I learned to connect with others on a deeper level, empathizing with their struggles and offering support and encouragement. This sense of community and connection became a powerful catalyst for my growth and healing.

Ultimately, my time in the treatment center taught me that true strength lies not in avoiding our emotions but in embracing them. I learned that by confronting our fears and vulnerabilities, we can uncover a sense of calm and clarity that enables us to access our inner strength. As Marcus

Aurelius so eloquently stated, "The nearer a man comes to a calm mind, the closer he is to strength."

Seneca Quote

As I reflect on my journey through the treatment center, I am reminded of the profound wisdom in Seneca's quote: "We suffer more in imagination than in reality." My experience has taught me that this phrase is not merely a philosophical concept, but a harsh reality that I had to confront directly.

Upon entering the treatment center, I was overwhelmed by the weight of my struggles. Substance abuse, anxiety, abandonment, and ADHD had significantly impacted my mental and emotional well-being. I felt as though I was drowning in a sea of self-doubt, fear, and shame. The prospect of confronting my demons was daunting, and I often questioned whether I possessed the strength to overcome them.

But as I embarked on my journey, I gradually came to understand that my greatest enemy was not the substances to whichI was addicted, nor the anxiety that tormented me, nor the abandonment issues that lingered in my mind. It was my own imagination. I had constructed a narrative about myself that was far more damaging than the reality of my circumstances.

I discovered that my anxiety was not a reflection of the world around me, but rather a manifestation of my own fears and worries. I realized that my abandonment issues stemmed not from the actions of others, but from my own feelings of self-abandonment. Additionally, I came to understand that my ADHD is not a curse, but rather a distinctive aspect of my personality that can be harnessed for positive outcomes.

Through therapy, group sessions, and self-reflection, I began to challenge my negative thought patterns and rewire my brain to focus on the present moment. I learned to recognize the difference between reality and imagination, and to let go of the latter. I also learned to be kind to myself, to practice self-compassion, and to celebrate my strengths.

The treatment center was not merely a facility for receiving care; it was a sanctuary where I could confront my innerdemons and rediscover my true self. It provided an environment in which I could learn to embrace my imperfections and find tranquility amidst the chaos.

As I reflect on my journey, I am reminded that Seneca's quote is not merely a philosophical concept, but a reality I have experienced firsthand. I have come to understand that I suffer more in my imagination than in reality, and this realization has empowered me to overcome my struggles.

I am grateful for the treatment center, the therapists, the group members, and the wisdom of Seneca. I appreciate the opportunity to confront my demons and rediscover myself. I am also thankful for the realization that I suffer more in my imagination than in reality, as it has empowered me to live a life that is authentic, meaningful, and free.

Chinese Proverbs

As I reflect on my time at the treatment center, I am reminded of the profound lessons I learned about myself and the significance of patience. The Chinese proverb, "A little impatience will spoil great plans, resonated deeply with me as I worked to overcome my anxiety, abandonment issues, addictions, and ADHD.

Upon my arrival, I was overwhelmed by the sheer magnitude of my problems. I felt as though I were drowning in a sea of self-doubt, shame, and fear. The anxiety was suffocating, making it difficult to breathe, think clearly, or even function. My Abandonment issues left me feeling unworthy of love and connection. My addictions had taken control, clouding my judgment and leading me down a path of destruction. Additionally, my ADHD made it challenging to focus, resulting in feelings of frustration and inadequacy.

But as I began the treatment process, I gradually started to untangle the complex threads of my psyche. I learned that patience is not merely a virtue but a necessity. I realized that hastening through the healing process would only result in further chaos and destruction. The therapists and counselors at the center taught me that recovery is a marathon, not a sprint.

One of the most significant lessons I learned was the importance of self-compassion. I realized that I had been my own worst critic, berating myself for every perceived mistake and shortcoming. I learned to be kind to myself, to acknowledge my struggles, and to celebrate my small victories. This newfound self-compassion enabled me to approach my challenges with a sense of curiosity and openness, rather than fear and resistance.

Another crucial lesson was the power of mindfulness. I learned to focus on the present moment rather than getting caught up in worries about the past or future. Mindfulness helped me stay grounded and centered, even amidst chaos. It allowed me to recognize my thoughts and emotions without becoming consumed by them.

The treatment center also taught me the importance of community and connection. I developed deep bonds with my fellow patients, who became a vital source of support and encouragement. We shared our struggles and triumphs, and I realized that I was not alone in my challenges. This sense of belonging and connection helped me feel less isolated and more empowered.

As I reflect on my time at the treatment center, I am grateful for the lessons I learned. I have come to understand that patience is not a weakness but a strength. It enables us to confront our challenges with clarity and intention, rather than hastily plunging into chaos. Additionally, I learned that recovery is a journey, not a destination. It demands continuous effort and commitment, but the rewards are immeasurable.

In the end, I learned that "A little impatience can spoil great plans." However, I also discovered that patience, self-compassion, mindfulness, and community can lead to a life filled with purpose, joy, and fulfillment.

Voltaire Quote

As I made my way to the New Tree Treatment Center in Laguna, California, I couldn't help but reflect on the journey that had led me to this moment. I thought about the struggles I had faced, the battles I had fought, and the scars I had accumulated along the way. However, as I sat in the waiting room, surrounded by the quiet hum of strangers seeking solace, I realized that I was not alone.

The amusing incident that occurred on my way to treatment was that I finally acknowledged the elephant in the room. This elephant had been hiding in plain sight, taunting me with its presence and whispering cruel nothings in my ear. It represented my struggles with addiction, ADHD, abandonment, and anxiety.

For far too long, I attempted to confront these demons on my own, relying on coping mechanisms that merely masked the pain. The truth is, I could not do it alone. I needed help, and I needed it immediately.

As I sat there, I reflected on the quote that had become my mantra: "Stupid is the man who always remains the same." Voltaire's words resonated in my mind, serving as a reminder that growth and change are the only constants in life. I understood that I had to be open to change.

Treatment would not be easy. It would be a journey of self-discovery, involving the confrontation of the darkest corners of my mind and the navigation of the complexities of my emotions. However, I was prepared. I was ready to face my demons head-on, to confront the lies I had told myself, and to learn to love myself for who I truly am, flaws and all.

As I left the treatment center that day, I experienced a sense of hope that I had not felt in years. I recognized that I still had a long journey ahead, but I also understood that I was not alone. I was part of a community of individuals who were facing the same struggles and were committed to doing the hard work necessary to overcome them.

And so, I continue on this journey, armed with the knowledge that I am not alone and that growth and change are always within reach. I am not the same person I was when I first entered that treatment center, and I am grateful for this transformation. I have learned that it is only by embracing our imperfections and being open to change that we can truly discover ourselves.

A Man In Progress

As I reflect on my journey through a treatment center for alcoholism, abandonment, anxiety, and ADHD, I am reminded of the profound lessons I learned. The experience was transformative, filled with challenges, setbacks, and triumphs. Mostimportantly, it taught me the value of perseverance and the power of self-acceptance.

One of the most significant takeaways was the understanding that progress is not always linear. I faced setbacks and relapses, but I learned to reframe them as opportunities for growth rather than failures. The phrase, matter how many mistakes you make or how slowly you progress, you are still way ahead of everyone who isn't trying, became a mantra for me. It reminded me that every step forward, no matter how small, is a victory.

The treatment center provided a safe environment where I could confront my demons and address my issues. I was surrounded by individuals who understood my struggles and were dedicated to helping me overcome them. The sense of community and support was tangible, giving me the courage to be vulnerable and honest about my feelings.

I also learned the importance of self-compassion. I had always been my own harshest critic, berating myself for perceived mistakes and shortcomings. However, during my time at the treatment center, I began to practice self-acceptance and self-forgiveness. I realized that I was doing the best I could with the resources available to me, and that was sufficient.

The treatment center taught me the importance of mindfulness and self-care. I learned techniques for managing my anxiety and ADHD, including meditation and deep breathing exercises. Additionally, I discovered the significance of addressing my physical and emotional needs, such as ensuring adequate sleep and maintaining a balanced diet.

Perhaps the most significant lesson I learned was the importance of self-awareness. I gained a deeper understanding of my thought patterns, emotions, and behaviors, as well as their interconnections. I learned to recognize my triggers and patterns and to develop strategies for managing them effectively.

My experience at the treatment center was transformative. It taught me the value of perseverance, self-acceptance, and self-awareness. I learned to reframe setbacks as opportunities for growth and to practice self-compassion and self-care. I am grateful for the experience and the lessons I learned, and I continue to apply them in my daily life.

Avoiding Arguments While Under the Influence

The devastating effects of substance abuse on relationships are a well-documented reality. When we are in the throes of addiction, our judgment becomes clouded, and our behavior increasingly erratic. One of the most destructive consequences of substance abuse is the damage it inflicts on our relationships, especially during conflicts.

When we are under the influence, we are more likely to lash out at those around us, often without considering the consequences of our words. This behavior can lead to hurtful and damaging arguments that leave deep emotional scars. Furthermore, the toll of substance abuse can make us more susceptible to mood swings, anxiety, and depression, which can further exacerbate conflicts.

The truth is that substance abuse is a slippery slope that can quickly spiral out of control. When we find ourselves in the throes of addiction, our thinking becomes clouded, and our decisions are often motivated by a desire to escape or numb our pain. This can result in reckless behavior, including arguments that we may later come to regret.

But there is hope for redemption. The first step toward recovery is acknowledging the harm that substance abuse has inflicted on our relationships. This requires a willingness to confront our own flaws and take responsibility for our actions. By doing so, we can begin to rebuild trust and work toward healing.

One of the most crucial steps in preventing arguments related to substance abuse is to seek help. Whether through therapy, support groups, or counseling, obtaining professional guidance can equip us with the tools and resources necessary to overcome addiction. Furthermore, surrounding ourselves with supportive loved ones who are willing to hold us accountable can serve as a powerful deterrent against destructive behavior.

Ultimately, the key to avoiding conflicts related to substance abuse is to prioritize our relationships and our well-being. By acknowledging the devastating effects of addiction and seeking help, we can begin to rebuild and restore our connections, working towards a brighter and healthier future.

The Process of Finding Purpose

The pursuit of purpose and mastery is a lifelong journey that demands dedication, resilience, and a willingness to confront the unknown. While some may discover their calling in a moment of epiphany, for most of us, it is a gradual process of self-discovery and experimentation. Through ongoing introspection and effort, we can unlock our true potential and lead a fulfilling life.

The key to discovering our purpose lies in exploring the skills and opportunities that align with our personalities and inclinations. This may involve trying new activities, taking calculated risks, and stepping outside our comfort zones. Through this process of experimentation, we can gain a deeper understanding of ourselves and the world around us, ultimately uncovering our unique strengths and passions.

However, this journey is not without its challenges. We may face setbacks, failures, and moments of self-doubt along the way. It is during these times that we must tap into our inner strength and resilience, reminding ourselves that the pursuit of purpose is a marathon, not a sprint.

Despite the obstacles, the rewards of this journey are immeasurable. When we live a life of purpose, we become more focused, motivated, and fulfilled. We are better equipped to navigate life's challenges and are more likely to make a positive impact on the world around us.

The pursuit of purpose and mastery is a lifelong journey that demands dedication, resilience, and a willingness to confront the unknown. It is through this continuous process of self-discovery and experimentation that we can unlock our true potential and lead a fulfilling life. By embracing our unique strengths and passions, and persevering through the challenges that arise, we can achieve our goals and make a meaningful contribution to the world.

These R The Days Of R Lives

As we embark on the journey of recovery from substance abuse, it is essential to recognize the profound impact of our words on our path forward. The words we speak are not mere sounds; they are seeds that have the power to cultivate growth, nourish hope, and shape our destiny. When we open our mouths, we are not simply expressing ourselves; we are actively creating the world around us.

In the midst of addiction, our words often become a tangled web of negativity, self-doubt, and despair. We may find ourselves ensnared in a cycle of self-pity, lamenting what we lack and fixating on the perceived shortcomings of others.

However, as we embark on the path to recovery, it is essential to redirect our focus from what we do not have to what we do possess. By recognizing and celebrating our strengths, we can begin to restore our sense of self-worth and confidence.

Redemption is not about erasing the past; rather, it is about embracing the present moment and using it as an opportunity to create a brighter future. When we focus on what we lack, we become mired in regret and resentment, which can hinder our progress and perpetuate feelings of hopelessness. Instead, by concentrating on what we possess—our resilience, our support systems, and our capacity for growth—we can begin to heal and move forward.

As we speak, we are not merely conveying information; instead, we are planting seeds of hope, forgiveness, and transformation. Our words possess the power to liberate us from the shackles of addiction and to usher in a new era of freedom and possibility. By choosing to focus on the positive, we can begin to rewire our brains and cultivate a sense of gratitude, compassion, and self-love.

In recovery, our words serve as a powerful tool for transformation. They can provide comfort, act as a beacon of hope, and remind us of our strength and resilience. By expressing words of encouragement, support, and empowerment, we can begin to reconstruct our sense of identity and purpose. We can start to view ourselves as capable, worthy, and deserving of love and respect.

As we continue on our journey of recovery, it is essential to remember that our words are not merely a reflection of our current state; rather, they serve as a declaration of our intentions and aspirations. By choosing to speak words of redemption, we are not only seeking forgiveness but also actively creating a new reality—one that is rooted in hope, compassion, and transformation.

The words we speak are not merely a means of communication; they serve as a powerful catalyst for change. As we embark on the journey of recovery from substance abuse, it is essential to recognize the profound impact our words have on our path forward. By focusing on what we possess rather than what we lack, and by choosing to express words of hope, forgiveness, and transformation, we can begin to create a brighter future—one filled with purpose, meaning, and redemption.

Seven Words of Recovery

As I embarked on this journey of recovery, I have come to realize that certain words act as beacons, guiding me toward a path of healing and growth. These words, though seemingly ordinary, possess extraordinary significance, serving as a constant reminder of the principles that keep me on the road to recovery.

First and foremost, **consistency** is a vital component of my recovery. It involves an unwavering commitment to my daily routine, the discipline to adhere to my treatment plan, and the resilience to confront setbacks directly. Consistency fosters trust, enabling me to cultivate a sense of security and stability, which are essential for navigating the unpredictable landscape of recovery.

Reliability is a term that resonates deeply with me. It embodies the assurance that I can depend on myself, my support system, and my treatment team to be there for me, regardless of the circumstances. This sense of reliability cultivates trust, enabling me to feel secure in the understanding that I am not alone on this journey.

Simplicity has become a guiding principle for me. It signifies that recovery does not need to be complicated or overwhelming. By breaking my goals into manageable, bite-sized tasks, I can concentrate on the present moment instead of becoming bogged down by the complexities of the future.

Relatability is a term that has gained new significance for me. It embodies the understanding that I am not alone in my struggles; others have traversed this path before me and have emerged stronger and wiser as a result. Relatability enables me to connect with others on a deeper level, fostering meaningful relationships that cultivate a sense of belonging and community.

Authenticity has become a guiding principle for me. It represents my commitment to being true to myself, embracing my flaws, and valuing my unique experiences and perspectives. Authenticity empowers me to be vulnerable, take risks, and remain open to growth and change.

Humility is a term that has gained new significance for me. It embodies the understanding that recovery is not a solitary journey; instead, it is a collaborative effort that necessitates a willingness to listen, learn, and adapt. Humility enables me to stay grounded, remain receptive to feedback and guidance, and acknowledge that I do not possess all the answers.

Finally, **efficiency** has become a guiding principle for me. It represents the understanding that recovery is not a destination but a journey that demands a willingness to adapt, pivot, and evolve. Embracing efficiency enables me to maintain focus prioritize my goals, and maximize my time and energy.

These seven words—consistency, reliability, simplicity, relatability, authenticity, humility, and efficiency—serve as guiding beacons on my path to recovery and growth. They remind me that recovery is a journey, not a destination, and that it requires a willingness to adapt, evolve, and remain true to myself. By embracing these principles, I can navigate the road to recovery, one step at a time.

The Road to Recovery

The road to recovery from alcohol addiction is a long and challenging journey; however, with a clear roadmap, individuals can navigate their way to sobriety. The first step is to establish a personal and meaningful goal, accompanied by a deadline. This tangible target serves as a beacon, guiding the individual through the darkest moments of withdrawal and temptation.

A well-structured plan is essential for achieving this goal. It involves more than simply quitting cold turkey; it requires a comprehensive strategy that addresses the physical, emotional, and psychological facets of addiction. This plan should incorporate a robust support system, which may include a therapist, a support group, or loved ones, to offer encouragement and accountability.

Consistent action is the key to fulfilling this plan. It is not about making grand gestures or experiencing epiphanies; rather, it involves taking small, incremental steps toward recovery. This may include attending daily meetings, practicing mindfulness, or engaging in healthy hobbies. The objective is to establish a sense of routine and normalcy, gradually replacing the patterns of addiction with new, healthier habits.

As individuals progress along the road to recovery, they will encounter setbacks and challenges. It is essential to be patient and compassionate with oneself, recognizing that relapse is a natural part of the process. Instead of viewing setbacks as failures, they should be seen as opportunities for learning and growth, allowing for the refinement of plants and adaptation to new circumstances.

The journey to sobriety is not merely about quitting alcohol; it is about rediscovering oneself. It involves uncovering the underlying issues that contributed to addiction and addressing them directly. This process may include exploring past traumas, building self-esteem, and developing effective coping mechanisms. The ultimate goal is to emerge from the darkness of addiction with a renewed sense of purpose and direction.

Ultimately, the road to recovery is a personal and unique journey. There is no one-size-fits-all approach; what works for one individual may not work for another. The key is to remain committed to the plan, be open to new experiences and perspectives, and celebrate small victories along the way.

As the individual approaches their deadline, they will begin to feel a sense of accomplishment and pride. They will realize that they have not only overcome their addiction but have also discovered a newfound sense of purpose and fulfillment. The road to recovery may be long and winding, but with a clear plan, consistent action, and a willingness to learn and grow, individuals can emerge from the darkness of addiction into the light of sobriety.

Mantra for Motivation

As I sat in the tranquility of my treatment room, I stumbled upon a quote that would forever alter the course of my journey: "Greatness is a decision. When I decide to be unstoppable, I am unbeatable." - Byron Allen. Those powerful words resonated deeply within me, like a spark igniting a flame.

In that moment, I realized that my recovery was not merely about overcoming addiction; it was about embracing a new mindset. It involved making the conscious decision to take control of my life, to become unstoppable, and to be unbeatable. I understood that I possessed the power to shape my own destiny, to rise above the challenges that lay ahead, and to emerge stronger and more resilient than ever before.

As I repeated those words to myself, I felt a surge of determination and motivation. I realized that I was not merelyfighting for my life, but for my freedom. I was choosing to break free from the shackles of addiction, to shatter the chains of self-doubt, and to unleash my true potential.

From that day forward, those words became my mantra, my guiding light, and my source of inspiration. Whenever I felt the urge to give up or sensed that I was losing my way, I would repeat those words to myself and find the strength to persevere.

I have come to understand that greatness is not merely a circumstance that befalls us; rather, it is a choice we make. It involves the decision to take risks, push boundaries, and pursue excellence. It is a commitment to being bold, fearless, and unstoppable.

As I continued my journey, I began to notice the subtle yet profound changes within myself. I felt more confident, empowered, and resilient. It was as if I could conquer the world, as though nothing could stand in my way.

And you know what? Nothing could stop me. I was unstoppable. I was unbeatable. I was a force to be reckoned with—aforce that could not be defeated.

So, to anyone who is struggling and fighting to overcome their own demons, I want to share Byron Allen's powerful words with you. Remember that greatness is a choice. When you choose to be unstoppable, you become unbeatable. You are a force to be reckoned with—a champion, a warrior, and a conqueror.

Repeat those words to yourself and witness your life transform before your very eyes. Observe as you rise above challenges, overcome obstacles, and emerge victorious.

The Quote of Sobriety

I still remember the day I stumbled upon a profound quote: "If you've forgotten the language of gratitude, you'll never be on speaking terms with happiness." It felt as though the words were speaking directly to my soul, resonating with the deepest struggles I was facing at that time. I was caught in a vicious cycle of substance abuse, and the message of the quote struck me like a ton of bricks.

As I read those words, I couldn't help but reflect on the countless times I had neglected to express gratitude for the small blessings in life. I had become so consumed by my addiction that I lost sight of the beauty and wonder that surrounded me each day. I had overlooked the love and support of my family and friends, the roof over my head, and the food on my table.

But as I reflected on the quote, something shifted within me. I realized that my addiction was not solely about the substances I was using; it was also about the profound emptiness and dissatisfaction I felt deep down. I was pursuing a high that I believed would bring me happiness, but it was only driving me further away from it.

The quote became a pivotal moment in my life. It prompted me to recognize the necessity of change and to begin incorporating gratitude and mindfulness into my daily routine. Acknowledging that I couldn't navigate this journey alone, I made the challenging decision to seek assistance at a substance abuse treatment center.

The journey was challenging, but ultimately rewarding. I learned to cultivate gratitude and self-awareness, and gradually,I began to experience a sense of happiness and fulfillment that I had never known before. I came to appreciate the smallthings, cherish the people and experiences that brought joy to my life, and find peace in the present moment.

Looking back, I realize that the quote was more than just a phrase—it was a wake-up call, a reminder that happiness is not something to be found in substances or external sources, but rather in the simple act of being grateful for what we already possess. It served as a reminder that happiness is a choice and that we have the power to cultivate it within ourselves.

Today, I am thankful for that quote and the journey it inspired. I appreciate the opportunity to learn and grow, as well asthe chance to discover happiness and fulfillment in a way that is both authentic and meaningful. I am also grateful for the reminder that happiness is always within reach, as long as we remember to embrace the language of gratitude.

Theater of The Mind

The human mind is a powerful instrument, capable of shaping our reality and influencing our actions. This idea has been explored by both philosophers and scientists, but the truth remains: our mind responds precisely to what it believes we desire, acting in accordance with our thoughts and commands. This concept is grounded in the fundamental principles of human nature, where our brains are wired to seek pleasure and avoid pain.

As I reflect on my journey, I realize that my mind was, in fact, steering my decisions and actions toward a path of self-destruction. The anxiety, alcohol, and ADHD felt like a three-headed monster, constantly whispering in my ear, "You're not good enough," "You're a failure," and "You're a burden." However, I understood that I needed to break free from this cycle of self-doubt and negativity.

The decision to seek treatment marked a pivotal moment in my life. It was a choice that demanded courage, vulnerability, and a readiness to confront the demons that had been holding me back. As I entered the treatment center, I experienced a mix of trepidation and a glimmer of hope. I understood that I was taking the first step toward redemption, toward reclaiming my life and my sanity.

The treatment center became a sanctuary—a place where I could confront my fears and insecurities in a safe and supportive environment. The therapists, counselors, and medical professionals worked tirelessly to help me untangle the complex threads of my mind, rewiring my brain and reprogramming my thoughts. It was a challenging journey, but one that was essential for my growth and healing.

As I progressed through treatment, I began to realize that my mind was, in fact, responding to my thoughts and commands. I was no longer a slave to my anxiety, alcohol, and ADHD; I was taking control of my life, one thought at a time. I learned to reframe my negative self-talk, challenge my distorted thinking patterns, and cultivate a sense of self-compassion and self-acceptance.

The journey was not without its setbacks; however, with each obstacle, I grew stronger, more resilient, and more determined. I began to recognize that my mind was capable of incredible feats and that it could be shaped and molded to achieve greatness. I realized that I possessed the power to choose my thoughts, emotions, and actions.

 My decision to seek treatment was a testament to the power of the human mind. It was a declaration of my willingness to take control of my life, confront my demons, and emerge victorious. As I reflect on my journey, I am reminded that my mind is a powerful tool, capable of shaping my reality and guiding my actions. I am grateful for the opportunity to have redeemed myself, reclaimed control of my life, and emerged stronger, wiser, and more compassionate.

Modern-Day Apprentice

As I sit here reflecting on my journey, I am overwhelmed with emotions. The road to sobriety has been long and arduous, yet the sense of accomplishment and freedom is indescribable. I am a modern-day apprentice, learning to navigate the complexities of my mind and emotions.

I was once overwhelmed by anxiety and depression, feeling as though I was drowning in a sea of uncertainty. The darkness was suffocating, and I felt as if I was losing myself in the process. I turned to alcohol as a coping mechanism, believing it would numb the pain and offer a temporary escape. However, as days turned into weeks and weeks into months, I realized that I was merely exchanging one addiction for another.

ADHD, a constant companion, made it challenging for me to concentrate and maintain focus. I felt trapped in a never-ending cycle of chaos, unable to find peace or clarity. The anxiety and depression only intensified, leading me to feel as though I was losing my grip on reality.

But something inside me clicked. I realized that I had a choice: to continue down the path of self-destruction or to take control of my life. I knew it wouldn't be easy, but I was determined to find a way out of the darkness.

I began my journey by seeking help. I attended therapy sessions, where I learned to confront my inner struggles and process my emotions. I started practicing mindfulness and meditation, discovering solace in the stillness and tranquility. Additionally, I began taking medication to help manage my ADHD, and gradually, I started to feel like myself again.

The journey has been anything but easy. There have been setbacks and challenges along the way, but I have learned to be kind to myself and to take things one step at a time. I have prioritized my well-being and have become more attuned to the needs of my body and mind.

As I reflect on my journey, I am filled with a profound sense of pride and accomplishment. I take pride in having facedmy fears and taken control of my life. I am also proud of my bravery in seeking help when I needed it most.

I am not the same person I was a year ago. I have become stronger, wiser, and more compassionate. I am now more aware of my emotions and better equipped to manage them. Additionally, I feel more confident and self-assured.

I am a modern-day apprentice, learning to navigate the complexities of my mind and emotions. I am a work in progress, but I take pride in the strides I have made. I am grateful to be alive and to live a life that is authentic to who I am.

Michael Joseph Jackson

The Moonwalk of Sobriety! As I reflect on my journey from addiction to recovery, I am reminded of the iconic albums "Off the Wall" and "Thriller" by the King of Pop, Michael Jackson. Just as MJ's music transcended genres and generations, my struggles with addiction and subsequent path to sobriety have been a tumultuous journey, filled with unexpected twists and turns.

Like "Off the Wall," my addiction resembled a thrill-seeking adventure, providing a rush of adrenaline that concealed the pain and emptiness within. I became ensnared by the allure of instant gratification, relishing the fleeting high that accompanied each fix. However, just as the album's title implies, I found myself trapped in a cycle, unable to escape the grip of addiction.

Then came the moment of reckoning, the epiphany that changed everything. I realized that my addiction was a monster, a force that was slowly devouring my life, my relationships, and my sense of self. I knew I had to confront the beast head-on, to face my demons and overcome them.

Sobriety was akin to the "Beat It" challenge—a test of resilience, a struggle to conquer the cravings and temptations that lurked around every corner. However, just as Michael Jackson's music inspired us to "Beat It," I realized that I possess the strength to overcome my addiction, to rise above the chaos, and to discover my inner fortitude.

Today, I am proud to declare that I am "Off the Wall from the constraints of addiction and embracing a life filled with purpose and meaning. My journey has been a ride, replete with twists and turns, but I have emerged stronger, wiser, and more resilient than ever.

My journey through addiction and sobriety resembles the music of Michael Jackson—a testament to the human spirit's capacity for transformation, growth, and resilience in the face of adversity. Just as MJ's music continues to inspire and uplift us, my story serves as a reminder that recovery is attainable; we can conquer even the darkest addictions and emerge victorious, much like the King of Pop himself.

Merchandise of Paradise: My Journey Through Addiction and Recovery**

As I reflect on my journey, I am reminded of the tantalizing allure of paradise—a place where every desire is fulfilled, every pain is erased, and every worry is silenced. For me, this paradise manifested in the form of substances, which promised to rescue me from the depths of despair and transport me into a world of euphoria. However, like a siren's song, their promise was a deception, and their reality became a never-ending cycle of addiction and destruction.

My addiction began innocently enough, serving as a means to cope with the stress and anxiety of everyday life. However, it quickly transformed into a crutch—a security blanket I felt I could not live without. I became convinced that I needed it to function, to feel normal, to be myself. Consequently, I continued to feed my addiction, even as it devastated my relationships, compromised my health, and eroded my very soul.

But there came a time when the paradise I had created began to unravel. The substances that had once brought me immense joy and relief now dominated my life, dictating every action I took, every thought I entertained, and every decision I made. I found myself ensnared in a relentless cycle of addiction, and I felt powerless to escape.

It was at that moment that I hit rock bottom. I had lost everything that mattered to me—my relationships, my job, my home, and even my sense of self. I was left with nothing but the bitter taste of regret and the crushing weight of my own failures.

And yet, it was in that darkest of places that I discovered the strength to embark on my journey toward sobriety. I realized that I had been living in a fantasy world of my own making, where substances had promised me a paradise that was never real. I began to understand that my addiction was not a solution but rather a problem

—a symptom of deeper issues that needed to be addressed.

Sobriety has not been easy. It has been a daily struggle, a constant battle to remain on the path and resist the temptations my old habits. However, it has also been a journey of self-discovery, growth, and healing. I have learned to confront my demons, face my fears, and find peace in the present moment.

As I reflect on my journey, I am reminded that the paradise I once sought was never real. It was a myth, a fantasy, a deception. However, the path to sobriety has been genuine, and it has been worthwhile. Ultimately, it is not the substances that bring us joy and fulfillment, but the connections we forge with others, the experiences we embrace, and the personal growth we attain.

The treasures of paradise are not found in a bottle of pills or a bag of powder, but in a life filled with purpose, meaning, and fulfillment. I am grateful to be living such a life, one day at a time.

Elevators

I have lived a life filled with turmoil, ensnared in a web of addiction, mental health challenges, and self-doubt. The films "Lift to the Scaffold" and "Elevator to the Gallows" resonate deeply with my personal struggles, serving as a reminder that I am not alone in this battle.

As I navigated the dark alleys of addiction, I found solace in the cinematic masterpiece "Lift to the Scaffold The film's protagonist, Flore, is a young woman ensnared in a world of desperation, much like I was during my struggles with alcoholism. Her story serves as a poignant reminder that we are all striving to find our way, seeking to escape the suffocating grip of our own demons.

But my struggles did not end with addiction. Depression, anxiety, and abandonment issues infiltrated my life, much like unwelcome guests at a party. I felt as though I were trapped in a never-ending elevator, ascending and descending without respite, burdened by the overwhelming weight of my own thoughts. It was as if I were ensnared in an unrelenting cycle of self-doubt, unable to muster the courage to take the next step.

And then, there was ADHD. The constant distractions, the inability to concentrate, and the sensation of being adrift in a sea of chaos. It felt as though I were trapped in an endless loop of noise, unable to find the silence I so desperately craved.

But here's the thing: I'm not alone. I have found solace in the films of Louis Malle, in the struggles of his characters, and in my own struggles. I have learned that even in the darkest of times, there is always hope. There is always a way out, always a chance to start anew.

As I reflect on my journey, I recognize that I have been bestowed with a rare gift—the gift of resilience. I have faced challenges that have left me broken, battered, and bruised, yet I have never surrendered. That, my friends, is the greatest victory of all.

So, to anyone grappling with addiction, depression, anxiety, abandonment issues, or ADHD, I want you to know that you are not alone. You are not a failure; you are not a lost cause. You are a warrior, a fighter, a survivor. You possess the strength to overcome, to rise above, and to find your path.

As I look to the future, I recognize that I will continue to encounter challenges. However, I am confident that I will confront them with courage, determination, and the understanding that I am not alone. That, my friends, is the greatest motivator of all.

Product of My Environment

The environment in which we grow up can profoundly impact our lives, shaping our thoughts, behaviors, and decisions. A negative environment, characterized by poverty, abuse, or neglect, can leave deep scars that persist long after we have escaped its confines. However, it is essential to acknowledge that our past does not have to dictate our present decision-making.

As someone who has battled addiction and is now on the path to recovery, I have come to appreciate the profound influence of our environment. Growing up in a dysfunctional household, I was exposed to toxic behaviors and attitudes that distorted my perception of reality. I believed I was worthless, that I did not deserve happiness, and that I was fated to a life of struggle.

But here's the thing: just because I grew up in a challenging environment doesn't mean I have to remain trapped in it. My past may have shaped me, but it doesn't have to dictate my future. I possess the strength to break free from the constraints of my upbringing and forge a new reality for myself.

In my journey of sobriety and recovery, I have learned that it is essential to acknowledge the past without allowing it to define me. I have confronted the demons that haunted me, faced the pain and shame, and learned to forgive both myself and others. Although it has been a long and arduous process, it has been worth every moment.

Today, I am proud to say that I am no longer controlled by my past. I have learned to recognize the triggers that once sent me spiraling into addiction, and I have developed coping mechanisms to manage them. I have built a support network of loved ones and peers who encourage and motivate me to stay on track. Additionally, I have discovered a sense of purpose and meaning that provides me with direction and fulfillment.

So, to anyone who is struggling with their own demons, I want to emphasize that you are not alone. Your past may have been challenging, but it does not define your worth. You possess the power to break free, to create a new reality, and to live a life that is authentic and meaningful.

Remember, while your environment may have influenced you, it does not have to define you. You possess the power to rise above challenges, overcome obstacles, and thrive. Take charge of your life, and refuse to let your past dictate your present. You are stronger than you realize, and you are capable of achieving greatness.

I am just a kid from 53206, a zip code often associated with poverty, violence, and despair. However, I am more than just a statistic. I am a survivor, a warrior, and a testament to the resilience of the human spirit, capable of overcoming even the darkest circumstances.

Growing up in the 53206 area, I was surrounded by trauma. I witnessed friends and family members fall victim to the streets, their lives tragically cut short by senseless violence. The sounds of gunfire and sirens filled the air, and their echoes continue to haunt my dreams. However, despite the chaos and destruction that permeated every aspect of my life, I refused to let it define me.

As a teenager, I resorted to substances to cope with the pain and anxiety that threatened to overwhelm me. I believed that by numbing my emotions, I could escape the harsh reality of my situation. However, I soon found myself ensnared in a cycle of addiction, using it to evade the very problems I was attempting to flee.

But then, something changed. I hit rock bottom and realized that I had two choices: I could continue down the path of self-destruction, or I could fight to reclaim my life. I chose the latter.

Recovery was not easy. It was a long and arduous journey, filled with setbacks and struggles. There were moments when I felt like giving up, when the pain and shame seemed unbearable. However, I refused to let my past define me. I sought help, found support, and began to rebuild my life.

Today, I am sober. I am in recovery, and I am proud. I take pride in the person I am becoming, the struggles I have overcome, and the hope I have discovered. I serve as a reminder that no matter where you come from or what you have experienced, you possess the power to change your narrative.

But my journey is not solely about myself. It encompasses the countless others who are struggling, suffering, and searching for a way out. It includes the children from 53206 and every other zip code who are fighting to overcome the trauma and pain inflicted upon them.

I am just a kid from 53206, but I also represent hope. I serve as a reminder that no matter what you have experienced, you are not alone. You are not defined by your past; you are capable of change, growth, and redemption.

So, to all the children from 53206 and to all the kids from every other zip code, I say this: don't give up. Don't lose hope. You are stronger than you realize, and you are capable of overcoming any challenges that come your way. Keep fighting, keep pushing, and never lose sight of the fact that you are deserving of love, life, and a second chance.

Shawn's Pen

The mighty pen has graced the page, and I am ready to "ink" a tale of redemption! I firmly believe that God has utilized my sobriety and recovery to "write" a new chapter in my life—one that is filled with purpose and meaning.

You see, my journey to sobriety was no easy feat. It was a tumultuous road, filled with twists and turns, ups and downs. However, as the saying goes, "when life gives you lemons, make lemonade." That's precisely what I did. I took those lemons and used them to enrich my soul.

As I navigated the ups and downs of recovery, I began to realize that God was using my struggles to shape me into the person He intended me to be. It was a process of chiseling away at my imperfections, refining me like gold in a furnace. Just as a masterpiece is revealed in the fire, my true self began to emerge.

But here's the thing: God doesn't only use the good times to shape us; He also utilizes the bad. Trust me, I've experienced my fair share of difficult days—days when I felt trapped in a rut, as if I were sinking deeper and deeper into quicksand. Yet, even in those darkest moments, God was working behind the scenes, using those experiences to mold me into the person He intended me to be.

And let me tell you, it has been a wild ride! Through it all, I have come to realize that God is a master craftsman, weaving together the threads of our lives to create a beautiful tapestry of purpose and meaning. I am not just referring to my own life; I am also speaking about the lives of those around me.

You see, when we find ourselves in the midst of a struggle, it's easy to feel isolated, as if we are the only ones experiencing such challenges. However, the truth is that we are not alone. We are all in this together, and God is using our struggles to connect us with one another, fostering a community of believers who can support and encourage each other along the way.

So, if you're experiencing a difficult time right now, remember that God is using it to "shape" you into the person He intends for you to become. He is molding you into a masterpiece, a work of art that is uniquely yours. Even amidst the struggle, He is connecting you to others, fostering a community of believers who can support and encourage you along the way.

At the end of the day, it all comes down to perspective. It involves viewing life's struggles as opportunities rather than obstacles. It requires trusting that God is using even our negative experiences to prepare us for future service and to enhance our potential for tomorrow. When we adopt this mindset, we will discover that our struggles become the foundation upon which our greatest triumphs are built.

The Closer

As I reflect on my journey of sobriety, living with ADHD, and overcoming trauma, I am reminded of the wise words of the Wiz : "You've had the power all along." This phrase has become a beacon of hope and resilience for me, guiding me through the darkest times and illuminating my path to healing.

I remember the countless nights I spent struggling to sleep, my mind racing with the demons of addiction and the weight of my past traumas. The sound of the clock ticking away, the creaks and groans of the old house, and the distant hum of the city outside seemed to echo the turmoil within me. It felt as though I was trapped in a never-ending cycle of self-doubt and fear.

But then, something shifted. I began to see the world through the lens of the Wiz, and suddenly, the power to change was within my grasp. I realized that I had been living in a world of my own making—a world of black and white, where the only colors were the shades of my addiction and trauma. However, the Wiz revealed to me that there was a world beyond, a world filled with vibrant colors, hope, and possibility.

As I embarked on my journey of sobriety, I encountered the challenges posed by ADHD. The constant distractions, racing thoughts, and impulsive behaviors often conflicted with my newfound commitment to recovery. However, the Wiz whispered in my ear, "You've had the power all along." I learned to harness my energy, channel my creativity, and utilize my impulsivity to propel me forward.

And then, there was the trauma. The memories, flashbacks, and nightmares served as constant reminders of the pain and suffering I had endured. However, the Wiz taught me that even in the darkest times, there is always a glimmer of hope. I learned to confront my demons, face my fears, and discover the strength to heal.

As I reflect on my journey, I am reminded of the Wiz's words: "You've had the power all along." This phrase has become a mantra for me, serving as a reminder that I possess the ability to shape my own destiny, create the life I desire, and overcome any obstacles that arise.

It's not about the destination; it's about the journey. It encompasses the struggles, setbacks, and triumphs. It involves the lessons learned, the growth experienced, and the wisdom gained. Moreover, it highlights the power that resides within each of us, waiting to be unleashed.

As I close this chapter of my life, I am filled with a sense of hope and gratitude. I am thankful for the lessons imparted by the Wiz and for the strength he revealed I possessed all along. I am eager to discover what the future holds, knowing that I have the ability to shape my own destiny and create a life filled with vibrant colors, hope, and endless possibilities.

The Epilogue of Trauma: A Journey of Sobriety, Recovery, and Unlikely Allies

As I stand before you today, I am reminded of the transformative power of resilience. My story encompasses trauma, addiction, and ultimately, recovery. However, it is not solely my own; it reflects the experiences of many who have traversed the same path. Remarkably, this narrative finds parallels in the characters of the beloved film "The Wiz."

Like Dorothy, I felt lost and disconnected from the world around me. The trauma I experienced as a child left me feeling as though I were trapped in a tornado, unable to find my way back to solid ground. However, just as Dorothy found her way to the Emerald City, I discovered a treatment center that became my sanctuary.

The journey to sobriety was not an easy one. It involved a daily struggle to confront the demons that haunted me and to face the pain and shame. However, with the support of my fellow travelers and the guidance of my therapists, I began to find my footing.

And then, there was the unexpected twist: the diagnosis of previously undiagnosed ADHD. It was as if the fog had lifted, allowing me to finally see the world with clarity. I realized that my struggles with addiction were not solely the result of trauma, but also stemmed from a neurological condition that had been misdiagnosed for years.

As I reflect on my journey, I am reminded of the characters from "The Wiz." There is the Scarecrow, who, despite lacking a brain, possesses a heart full of kindness and compassion. There is the Tin Man, who, despite his rusted exterior, has a soul that beats with empathy and understanding. And there is the Cowardly Lion, who, despite his fears, finds the courage to roar.

In the treatment center, I discovered my own Scarecrow, Tin Man, and Cowardly Lion. Each of us was broken in our own way, yet we were all seeking a path to healing. We found comfort in one another's presence, and together, we created a community that was greater than the sum of its parts.

As I reflect on my journey, I am reminded that recovery is not a solitary endeavor. It is a collective effort, a community of individuals who have traversed the same path and can provide a helping hand, a listening ear, or a comforting word.

And so, I encourage you to discover your own Scarecrow, Tin Man, and Cowardly Lion. Seek out your tribe, your community, and your support system. Just as Dorothy found her way back to

New York, you too can find your way back to yourself.

My story encompasses trauma, addiction, and recovery. However, it is also a narrative of hope, resilience, and the strength of community. As I look out at all of you, I am reminded that we are not alone on this journey. We are all in this together, and together, we can overcome even the most formidable challenges.

Miracles and Blessings,

SCW

BY
SHAWN CHRISTOPHER WILLIAMS

Caption

About the Author

Shawn Christopher Williams   Shawn Christopher Williams is a multifaceted individual with a proven track record of empowering communities and fostering positive change. As a skilled community connector, facilitator, conflict resolution mediator, and renowned community organizer, Shawn has dedicated his life to improving the lives of those around him.

Born and raised in Milwaukee , Wisconsin Shawn is a proud alumnus of Morris Brown College, a historically black college and university. This formative experience instilled in him a deep commitment to uplifting and supporting marginalized communities, particularly those impacted by systemic inequality and oppression.

Shawn's professional journey has taken him to various roles, each one building upon the last.

As an exegesis teller, he has honed his ability to listen deeply and empathetically, creating a safe space for individuals to share their stories and work through their challenges. This skill has served him well in his role as a conflict resolution mediator, where he has helped countless individuals and groups find common ground and resolve disputes in a peaceful and constructive manner.

As a community organizer, Shawn has been instrumental in mobilizing communities to address social and political issues. He has worked tirelessly to build coalitions, mobilize resources, and advocate for policies that promote justice, equity, and inclusion. His dedication to this work has earned him a reputation as a leader and a champion for marginalized communities.

Shawn's commitment to community building and empowerment extends beyond his professional work. He is an active member of his local community, volunteering his time and energy to support local organizations and initiatives. He is also a sought-after speaker and workshop facilitator, sharing his insights and expertise with audiences across the country.

Throughout his career, Shawn has been recognized for his outstanding contributions to community building and social justice. He has received numerous awards and accolades,.

Shawn Christopher Williams is a true servant leader, dedicated to empowering communities and fostering positive change. His tireless work and unwavering commitment to justice have made a profound impact on countless lives, and his legacy will continue to inspire and motivate future generations.